SECRET AMERICA

A GUIDE TO THE WEIRD, WONDERFUL, AND OBSCURE

David Baugher

Library of Congress Control Number: 2017935721

ISBN: 9781681061238

Design by Jill Halpin

Insert photo credits:

Hog Wild: San Juan Island National Historical Park

A Little Green: Portland Parks & Recreation

Car-Free is Carefree: Anastasia Klimovitz courtesy Mackinac Island Tourism Bureau

"Nobody Shot Me": Courtesy of the Mob Museum

Frozen Dead Guy Days: Andrew Wyatt with permission by Frozen Dead Guy Days

Meeting at the Tripoint: April Abel/Delaware State Parks

All Quiet on the West Virginia Front: National Science Foundation/Associated Universities, Inc./Green Bank Observatory

Biking the Apocalypse: Murray Schrotenboer

No Holier Place: Fort Sumter National Monument

"Planted up to the Very Door": Rachel Larue/Arlington National Cemetery

Life on the Line: John Fox/Courtesy of the Haskell Free Library

Man of the People: David Baugher

Printed in the United States of America

17 18 19 20 21 5 4 3 2 1

For my mother,
who taught me to look at the world differently

CONTENTS

INTRODUCTION

Where can one acquire an official NSA coffee mug? How was North Carolina almost annihilated in a nuclear explosion? Why does a federal court ruling prohibit Burger King from operating in Mattoon, Illinois? Was a major section of Boston once destroyed by molasses? Can you walk to Siberia from Alaska? Is the State of California named after a bad romance novel? What city are the real Monopoly properties in?

I love to ask questions about America and everyone loves a good secret. From finding out where Captain Kirk's future birthplace is located to exploring the hidden room behind Abe Lincoln's head on Mt. Rushmore, *Secret America* tells stories about the people, the places, the history, and the culture of some of the most obscure parts of our nation. Some of them will chill you to the bone, while others will warm your heart. And a good chunk of what's inside may just make you chuckle. Whether you want to stay at an underwater hotel beneath a Florida bay, attend a festival celebrating a frozen corpse in a Colorado town, or listen to Jerry Springer getting folksy at a Kentucky coffeehouse, you can find it all right here.

From the first atomic blast zone to the birthplace of college football, *Secret America* isn't easy to define, but it is fascinating to explore. It is a tourist guide for the hanging threads from the tapestry we call America, a collection of the individuals you didn't know existed, the places you didn't realize you could go, and the questions you never thought to ask.

Whether trying to enliven a family vacation or marveling at the amazing parallels of history, *Secret America* can take you from the planet's largest rural truck stop (seventy-five acres) to its smallest urban park (two feet across), from Nebraska's tiniest town to the Big Apple's busiest intersection, from a pyramid on the plains of North Dakota to a desert among the pine forests of Maine. This is the book that lets you explore the country with fresh eyes, taking in all the oddities and awesomeness you never understood were right under your nose.

1

<u>1</u> RIGHT ANGLES IN THE WRONG SPOT

Is the famous Four Corners monument in the wrong place?

It may not boast much in the way of tourist amenities but, if map nerds had a sacred site, this would be it. A quarter-million people a year make the pilgrimage along U.S. Route 160 to this scrubby patch of high desert to pay their respects to a place made remarkable not by history or nature but only by atlases and man's fascination with drawing lines. The Four Corners is the sole place in the United States—and one of the few in the world—where four borders meet as though set on a compass rose, with the delineations between Arizona, Utah, Colorado, and New Mexico rolling out from a disc-shaped monument ever-packed with cartographical tourists who contort themselves into pretzels so they can say they've officially put a limb in each state.

But did they really? Prepare yourself for a shock: the Four Corners monument is not in the right spot. Thanks to the vagaries of 19th-century surveying techniques, it is actually off by about 1,800 feet.

It is hard to conceive of it now, but back when state borders were being drawn, not everyone had GPS and an iPhone, so a surveyor's job was sometimes as much an art as a science, particularly when tracking through the wilderness. That's why so many supposedly "straight" borders of the boxy Western states actually have weird

---

Originally sited with a sandstone structure, the monument currently in use was built in 1992.

Borders aren't always the exact science we think they are, and these may not be quite where you think they are. Credit: Pixabay

THE FOUR CORNERS

WHAT A unity of states

WHERE The New Mexico–Colorado–Utah–Arizona border (or pretty close to it)

COST $5 per person

NOTEWORTHY Media reports and some pop culture sources have claimed that the monument is misplaced by more than two miles, but these rumors are false.

little jogs or sloping diagonals in them when viewed close up with the help of satellites.

That was certainly true for Chandler Robbins, the poor fellow saddled with the thankless task of divvying up the land. His measurements didn't quite come out exact, being inaccurate by about a third of a mile or so. That may seem demanding, yet—for a monument dedicated to exactitude—it would seem a tad disappointing to be off by more than a couple of football fields.

But fear not. If you are one of the hordes of tourists who have played impromptu games of Twister on the Four Corners monument, the National Oceanic and Atmospheric Administration's National Geodesic Survey (NOAA-NGS) says your exertions weren't in vain. According to the high poo-bahs of all matters mapworthy, the physical placement of the official marker defining the famous quadripoint supersedes any later nitpickery brought about by better technology. In short, if the monument says that's the spot where the states meet, then that's the spot where the states meet—whether it was supposed to be or not. Much like beauty, borders are in the eye of the beholder.

2 ARMAGEDDON IN WAYNE COUNTY

How was North Carolina nearly destroyed in a nuclear holocaust?

Wayne County, North Carolina, has all the attractions one might hope for. There is a local winery, plenty of tasty Southern barbecue, and an athletic park to work off any calories from partaking in the foregoing. There's even the obligatory Civil War historic locale with an interpretive walk showing one of the battlefields from a raid by Union Gen. George Foster.

And finally—if you have time—there is a small sign commemorating where a nuclear weapon almost irradiated the Eastern Seaboard.

This terrifying anecdote from the annals of Secret America occurred on January 23, 1961, when a pair of four-megaton hydrogen bombs were on a "routine" flight that became significantly less routine when the B-52 carrying them broke apart over the area and one of the devices began dutifully arming itself on its way back to Earth. Incredibly, three of the four safety interlocks went weapons-free, and the only thing that kept the payload from detonating with a force equivalent to 260 Hiroshimas and spreading fallout across the mid-Atlantic states was a single switch that Eric

---

THE GOLDSBORO INCIDENT SIGN

WHAT A new meaning for the term "North Carolina barbecue"

WHERE Main St. at Faro Rd. in Eureka, NC

COST A case of uncontrollable shudders

NOTEWORTHY The 1996 action thriller *Broken Arrow* was named for the military's term for a lost nuclear weapon.

Schlosser, author of *Command and Control: The Damascus Accident and the Illusion of Safety*, noted "was later found in some cases to be defective."

But apparently, it worked that day.

Had it not, radiation from the blast could potentially have spread as far afield as New York City. Sadly, three crewmen perished in the crash, but the effects could have impacted millions.

Moreover, the whole affair, eventually dubbed the Goldsboro Incident, wasn't as unusual as you might think. Schlosser, whose book should not be read by anyone wishing to ever enjoy a good night's sleep again, found that in less than two decades following 1950, the nation accumulated an impressive seven hundred "significant" incidents involving nuclear weapons.

Anyway, the actual site of the near-Armageddon is on private property but you can grab a quick selfie in nearby Eureka at the commemorative historical marker, which was erected just a few years ago after newly declassified documents came to light showing how close we came to only having one Carolina.

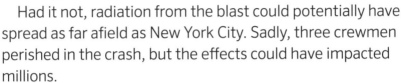

In 1980, an Arkansas explosion tossed a nine-megaton bomb an alarming distance after a chain of events that began when a workman in a silo accidentally dropped his wrench onto an ICBM.

CAR-FREE IS CAREFREE

Where can I visit a highway that prohibits cars?

Just as every state in Secret America comes with its own oddities, every state route comes with its own rules of the road. Still, any traveler on Michigan's Highway 185 is bound to notice that this roadway stands in a class by itself. "M-185" has the unusual distinction of being the sole state highway in the nation that bans motor vehicles.

Tucked neatly between the upper and lower peninsulas of Michigan, this eight-mile, two-lane loop of pavement rings scenic Mackinac Island near the northern edge of Lake Huron. It has official signage and designation from the state's Department of Transportation, and it even appears on Google Maps Street View—as does much of the island's car-free road system. In fact, motorized conveyances have been legally barred from the island since around the turn of the last century. Preferred modes of transportation include bikes, horses, and—of course—your own two legs. About four-fifths of Mackinac is a state park, but there is also a town and people do reside on this four-square-mile plot of terra firma just a short ferry ride from the automobile-saturated mainland. But don't be surprised to find that the neat rows of homes are missing driveways.

There's even a fair amount of folksy military history in this part of the Wolverine State. The French were the first Europeans to claim the area, but the British eventually took control and relocated their fort from the nearby

---

Don't forget to check out the nearby Mackinac Bridge, a five-mile span along I-75 that connects the two peninsulas of Michigan.

There is no rush hour on this highway—just lovely views. Credit: Anastasia Klimovitz courtesy Mackinac Island Tourism Bureau

and similarly named Fort Michilimackinac to the more cozy and defensible confines of the island in 1780. The Brits gave up their outpost to the fledgling United States only to return with unpleasant intent in 1812 and retake the island from an unfortunate American commander, Porter Hanks. Hanks was caught by surprise in the attack since a communications snafu with Washington, D.C., had left him unaware his country had gone to war. Hanks would eventually be charged with cowardice for the bloodless surrender of his fort in what would turn out to be the very first land engagement of the war. Regrettably, the luckless lieutenant would never get his day in court. He was killed by British artillery while awaiting trial inside a besieged Fort Detroit.

MICHIGAN'S HIGHWAY 185

WHAT A part of Secret America guaranteed to be free of speed traps

WHERE Mackinac Island, MI

COST Two ferries serve the island, and bikes are available for rent. Consult www.mackinacisland.org/stay/getting-here for more information.

NOTEWORTHY The island's Grand Hotel was shown in the 1980 time-travel/romance film *Somewhere in Time* with Christopher Reeve and Jane Seymour.

<u>4</u> A SPITEFUL SPIKE

Why did rail-grading crews pointlessly work past each other for 250 miles rather than connect at the Golden Spike?

Any student of U.S. history knows the tale. Two crews of sledge-driving men lay track across rugged mountain and wild prairie from both sides of the still-growing nation until, on a fateful day in 1869, the Union Pacific and the Central Pacific finally conquered an untamed continent by connecting east with west in a grand testament to the American spirit.

But there are problems with this romantic version of the story. For starters, the race to connect owed far less to the nobility of "can-do" Americanism and far more to pettiness and greed. That's the big reason the two petulant enterprises initially passed each other rather than meet and complete the job.

We often forget that the two companies laying track were not in fact partners engaged in a single grand project with a unified goal. They were in fact bitter rivals who utterly detested one another. Moreover, they had good reason. The government shelled out handsomely for each mile of track laid and the longer each side's contribution to the finished line, the greater control they had over local towns, ridership, and resources. Ironically, this actually provided something of a disincentive for the two enterprises to link up, and each kept sending grading crews to run further ahead, eventually working parallel—or even on top of—grading work done by the other.

The original Golden Spike is housed at the Cantor Arts Center at Stanford University.

This is where two competing rail enterprises were forced to meet. They weren't happy about it. Credit: David Baugher

THE GOLDEN SPIKE SITE

WHAT A spike driven into the heart of your notions about railroad history

WHERE Promontory Summit, UT

COST $5 for a private, non-commercial vehicle in winter ($7 in summer)

NOTEWORTHY Just after the turn of the last century, a new trestle made the Golden Spike line mostly obsolete to cross-country traffic, and trains stopped running there altogether by WWII.

"There is considerable opposition between the two railroad companies," noted one letter to a local newspaper. "Both lines run near each other, so near that in one place, the U.P. are taking a four feet cut out of the C.P. fill to finish their grade, leaving the C.P. to fill the cut thus made. . . ."

The close quarters didn't breed friendship, either. The writer went on to note the competing blasting crews' unneighborly habit of not always bothering to warn each other of impending detonations.

All of this attempted one-upsmanship led to lots of superfluous side-by-side grading work all the way into Nevada, with each company trying to gain an advantageous claim over the other until eventually Congress threatened to step in to stop the squabbling. Faced with the unpleasant prospect of government intervention, the U.P. and C.P. finally agreed reluctantly to a site where the Golden Spike could be driven and their historic competition could end.

5 THE KING OF MATTOON

Why does the federal government prohibit a prominent fast food chain from opening restaurants within twenty miles of a small Illinois town?

Taking a back seat only to McDonald's, Burger King is among the undisputed heavyweights of the fast-food universe. The home of the Whopper has brought its flame-grilled goodness to over ninety-one nations with more than 13,000 locations for patrons to chow down. From Bangladesh to Brazil, from Poland to Puerto Rico, the King reigns supreme.

But there is one place on Earth you won't find any of the famous chain's locations. That's within a twenty-mile radius of tiny Mattoon, Illinois.

That's no oversight. Thanks to a 1968 federal appeals court ruling, the Burger King chain is not allowed in Mattoon.

This tasty section of Secret America stems from local couple Gene and Betty Hoots, who owned an ice cream shop named Frigid Queen in the 1950s. When they wanted to expand their repertoire to hot food, a moniker for the new restaurant suggested itself immediately and the pair opened an eatery titled Burger King—completely unaware that a restaurant of that name already existed and was beginning its rapid expansion through the American South.

By 1961, the issue had come to a head when Burger King—the bigger one—arrived in the Land of Lincoln.

Mattoon, Illinois is home to the only Burger King in the country where you cannot have a Whopper. Credit: David Baugher

The chain had been using the name longer and had it federally protected, but the Hoots had a valid state-level trademark in Illinois. It wasn't long before the resulting court fight got hotter than a basket of fresh french fries.

Eventually, American jurisprudence arrived at a Solomonic compromise in the fast-food fiasco and split Illinois between Mattoon and . . . well . . . everywhere else, ruling that the Burger King chain could not legally open a restaurant within a twenty-mile radius of the Hoots' establishment.

According to local media reports, Betty Hoots said that the chain even offered ten grand to them for the right to move into town, but the couple "told them to get lost."

But Gene did make one allowance for his old rival.

"I like their food much better than McDonald's," he said.

In her youth, Sarah Michelle Gellar, best known for *Buffy the Vampire Slayer,* was a spokesgirl for Burger King in ads attacking Mickey D's burgers. She was even named in a lawsuit by the Golden Arches over the content of the ads she did—despite the fact that she was five years old at the time.

6 A TRUE TRIPLEHEADER

How did two Major League Baseball teams lose the same game?

Baseball is a sport that lends itself to oddities, but anyone who sat in the stands of New York's long-gone Polo Grounds on June 26, 1944, must have known they were witnessing probably the most bizarre game ever hosted on a diamond—one so complicated that it quite literally necessitated the use of a mathematician and a slide rule.

In short, what they saw was probably the sole example ever staged of a three-way baseball contest.

The idea, which gave new meaning to the term "tripleheader," was actually a philanthropic stunt designed to support war bond sales during WWII. All three Big Apple teams from the era participated, and the Giants, Dodgers, and Yankees squared off, with each one batting and fielding against alternating opponents. And thanks to the arithmetic artistry of Columbia University's Paul Smith, the contest didn't require twenty-seven innings. In fact, it was completed in the standard nine, with each side getting six innings of play and three on the bench.

But the day provided logistical challenges beyond simply figuring out which team got to bat next or how to draw up a tri-level box score without it looking weird. (Answer: you can't.) For one thing, the Dodgers and Yankees had to

---

The first officially recorded baseball game—a four-inning contest played in 1846 in Hoboken, New Jersey—was also between two Big Apple teams, with the New York Nine getting the win 23–1.

One can only imagine what the box score must have looked like for the game played on June 26, 1944 between three different teams.
Credit: Pixabay

share the same dugout, even in innings where they were playing against each other.

As for the scoring, it mostly required only one team. The Dodgers plated a run in the first against the Yankees and brought in two more in the second versus the Giants en route to an impressive 5-1-0 win. The Yankees managed to bring in a single tally in the ninth off the Giants, who garnered only two hits off either team. Ironically, the Dodgers—who were scheduled to sit out the ninth anyway—had already left the park to catch a train by the time they won the historic event.

THE POLO GROUNDS TOWERS

WHAT The site of the world's weirdest baseball game

WHERE Polo Grounds Towers, New York, NY

COST The ticket takers are long gone

NOTEWORTHY The Brooklyn Dodgers—now in Los Angeles—were originally named for their fans' aptitude for "dodging" electric trolleys which, in the 1890s, were an increasing cause of death for early pedestrians unaccustomed to looking both ways before crossing the street.

Anyway, while the Polo Grounds met the wrecking ball in 1964, there is still some evidence of its existence, including a plaque marking the location of home plate and two historic staircases—all of which can be found at the appropriately named Polo Grounds Towers, an apartment complex that sits along Frederick Douglass Boulevard near the Harlem River.

7 BARGAIN HUNTING AT THE NSA

Does America's most secretive agency have a gift shop?

Almost anyone would agree that the National Security Agency has had its share of public relations problems. In fact, until leaks from whistleblower Edward Snowden, few even knew this agency existed for the public to have relations with. Even the letter President Harry Truman wrote to help bring the NSA into existence in 1952 was officially classified. With a far lower public profile than its cloak-and-dagger cousin, the Central Intelligence Agency, the NSA has long operated in the shadowy universe of electronic eavesdropping with a reputation for secrecy so intense that its acronym earned the sobriquet "No Such Agency."

Today, it is perceived in popular culture as an enigmatic enterprise whose global reach evokes an edge of dark conspiracism inviting dystopian imagery and raising troubling questions about the elusive nature of privacy in the murky twilight intersection between technology, secrecy, and the nature of individual rights in an uncertain and dangerous world.

But, on the bright side, there is some cool stuff at the gift shop.

Well, of course, they have a gift shop. By God, this is America.

It is not just logoed coffee mugs either. You can also get

THE NATIONAL CRYPTOLOGIC MUSEUM

WHAT That's on a need-to-know basis

WHERE Colony Seven Rd., Fort Meade, MD

COST Free

NOTEWORTHY The NSA's insignia shows a bald eagle with a shield with its feet perched upon a key.

Now housed in the National Cryptologic Museum, this FROSTBURG supercomputer was once part of the National Security Agency. According to the museum's Facebook page, the flashing red lights actually have a functional purpose and were not added to make the computer look as cool as the one in the movie WarGames. Credit: Patrick Finnegan via Flickr under Creative Commons 2.0

NSA baseball caps, martini glasses, stuffed animals, and even a Magic 8-Ball—all emblazoned with insignia for America's most mysterious bureaucracy. *Business Insider* published a 2016 photo of the front window showing a sign saying that "the National Security Agency will neither confirm nor deny the accuracy" of any print or other media sold there. Yes, that's right. The NSA disavows items in its own gift shop. Cue the self-destructing audio tape.

In a 2013 *Washington Post* article, author James Bamford speculated that the NSA has enough data storage for five hundred quintillion pages of information. That's a five followed by twenty zeros.

Anyway, the shop is associated with the National Cryptologic Museum which, as the most public arm of the agency, is also something of a throwback to its roots in codebreaking institutions and practices going back to the Civil War. According to the website, about 50,000 visitors come through here annually to see exhibits detailing humanity's exhausting efforts to hide things and its equally energetic attempts to find out what exactly those things are. There are even tours, suggested programs for school field trips, and an extensive library on the science of codes and codebreaking.

The whole thing is highly educational and set next to something called the National Vigilance Park, which shows off reconnaissance aircraft. For students of history, the whole shebang looks remarkably interesting, though the website does note that the park is temporarily shut down to make way for a "visitor control center," which I'm certain is not meant to sound nearly as Orwellian as it does.

All jokes aside, the place looks remarkably intriguing and should be a great experience for fans of communications, espionage, and the fascinating universe of cryptology.

Plus, you can impress your friends by sipping casually from an NSA coffee mug during lunch. If they ask, you should look furtively back and forth, lean in, and whisper that you just got a great part-time job but you really aren't allowed to talk about it.

Then tell them to avoid speaking directly into the mug.

Other items at the museum show equipment used in cryptology. Credit: Patrick Finnegan via Flickr under Creative Commons 2.0

OF FRIENDSHIP AND FIREBOMBS

Why was the only enemy pilot to ever drop bombs on the mainland United States declared an honorary citizen by the town he attacked?

WWII fears of Japanese assault from the air weren't necessarily baseless. As proof, one need look no further than Nobuo Fujita. On September 9, 1942, the young Japanese pilot took off from a submarine in the Pacific and achieved the unique distinction of becoming the sole person in history to ever bomb the mainland United States from an enemy aircraft.

And apparently, he felt so terrible about it that he was ready to kill himself.

The remarkable story stems from Fujita's floatplane flight into coastal Oregon, where his mission was to drop two firebombs on a local wooded area and start a forest fire.

As for Fujita himself, his actions after the war ultimately opened a remarkable postscript to what would otherwise be nothing more than a bit of military trivia. As it turns out, twenty years after his historic bombing run, the ex-pilot was invited to visit the United States by the good people of Brookings, a town in the area hit by the incendiary devices. According to his daughter, quoted in his *New York Times* obituary, Fujita came prepared, even bringing along his family's four-hundred-year-old samurai sword with the

---

No other planes from Japan attacked the mainland, but at least two subs from that nation did shell points on the West Coast, though little damage was done.

the forest near Brookings, September 9, 1942.

Nobuo Fujita was the only enemy to bomb the U.S. ... in the air. He presented this sword during the 1962 ... which he and his family attended as guests of the Brookings Harbor Junior Chamber of Commerce.

This symbolic sword was presented in the interest of Peace and friendship between the nations of Japan and the United States of America.

The personal value of the ancestral sword to Mr Fujita attests to the sincerity of his gesture.

Nobuo Fujita's sword remains on display at the local library as a symbol of friendship between a pilot and the town whose forest he once bombed. Credit: Courtesy Chetco Community Public Library

NOBUO FUJITA'S SWORD

WHAT A symbol of friendship

WHERE Chetco Community Public Library, 405 Alder St., Brookings, OR

COST None

PRO TIP An interpretive sign can still be found marking the bombing site on Forest Trail #1118. Take U.S. Route 101 to the S. Bank Chetco River Rd. Head east to Mt. Emily Rd. (Forest Rd. 1205) for thirteen miles to the trailhead.

intent—should it become necessary—of disemboweling himself to make amends with the local residents.

Fortunately, he received a warm welcome from the townspeople, who were apparently not interested in a ritual suicide. Instead, they accepted the sword as Fujita's gift.

That event led to future visits to the town, as well as a $1,000 gift from Fujita to purchase books about Japan for the library. Fujita would even go on to plant trees in the forest he once tried to burn down.

In 1997, as Fujita lay on his death bed, Brookings declared him an honorary citizen of the town.

Today, Fujita's sword remains on display at the local library, a testament to the power of friendship between old enemies and one of the more heartwarming tales to emerge from Secret America.

9 A STROLL TO SIBERIA

Can you walk from America to Russia?

Vice-presidential candidate Sarah Palin once famously bragged that there were spots in her home state of Alaska from which one could see Russia. She took a lot of heat for the comment, which was widely spoofed on *Saturday Night Live* as "I can see Russia from my house."

However, Palin was correct. There are places in Alaska from which our Eurasian neighbor is visible. But could you walk there?

The surprising answer is yes, and it has actually been done. In 1998, a Russian father-son duo wearing skis accomplished the feat by trekking across the frozen Chukchi Sea at the north end of the Bering Strait. In addition to braving the elements for a stroll across the icy wastes of the Arctic for more than three weeks, the pair ran out of food, had to ward off an ill-tempered polar bear, and even broke through the ice at one point, which, father Dmitry Shparo told the *Juneau Empire,* made it impossible to dry his boots.

"Fortunately, it was not very cold," he said of the 150-mile trek across a frozen ocean in wet footwear.

LITTLE DIOMEDE

WHAT A walk to remember

WHERE Alaska

COST Safety, comfort, and possible arrest

PRO TIP Don't try this at home—or in Alaska, for that matter.

The narrowest point between the mainlands of Asia and North America is fifty-five miles.

Living on Little Diomede Island is about the closest you can actually get to seeing Russia from your house. Our Cold War-era opponent is less than three miles away from the spot. Credit: Alaska Department of Commerce, Community and Economic Development; Division of Community and Regional Affairs' Community Photo Library

But even Shparo's achievement pales in comparison to the wanderings of Karl Bushby, who, since 1998, has been attempting to walk from Chile to his hometown in Britain, a 36,000-mile journey across four continents that he has undertaken for remarkably nebulous reasons.

"The question of why is not easy," he said when asked about his epic stroll, which has included run-ins with Panamanian jungles, Colombian insurgents, Russian police, and American thieves.

He also crossed the strait, making it to the Chukotka Autonomous District, where he was briefly arrested. That brings up another problem with walking to Russia. It is illegal without proper paperwork.

Anyway, the best bet for a jaunt from the Land of the Free into Siberia is probably between the Big and Little Diomede Islands. At two-and-a-half miles apart, they are in separate nations.

Moreover, if you do take the big stroll, it will probably take you into tomorrow—literally. By crossing the International Date Line, where the global progression of time zones resets itself, your 2.5-mile walk will shift you twenty-one hours ahead.

But if you wish to simply stick to viewing Russia Palin-style, there are said to be some elevated points, such as St. Lawrence Island, where such a feat is possible when the fog isn't too bad. There really are places in the United States where you can see far enough to get a look at tomorrow.

10 "PLANTED UP TO THE VERY DOOR"

Did the United States' most sacred national cemetery begin as a form of revenge towards a general?

Arlington National Cemetery has sometimes been called America's most hallowed ground and, for the 4 million who visit it each year and the hundreds of thousands of honored military dead who lie beneath its soil, the title is no exaggeration. This is a place of deep reverence and eternal rest for heroes who gave all.

But the location of this sacred spot is no accident and its history bespeaks roots in a $92 tax bill, a multi-year legal fight, and what may perhaps be one of the single most creative acts of revenge in history.

The story stretches back to the onset of the Civil War, before which Arlington was originally the family estate of Mary Lee, wife of the famed Southern General Robert E. Lee. Being on the outskirts of Washington, D.C., the mansion and its grounds were seized without opposition by Union troops within hours of Virginia's declaring independence but, strictly speaking, Mary Lee still owned the property—even if she was now owning it from Richmond, the capital of the Confederate States of America, whose armies her husband led in the field.

To remedy this issue, the U.S. government devised a special tax that it assessed upon Arlington to the tune of $92.07. Further, it asserted that said tax had to be paid

---

The first man buried at Arlington, a private named William Christman, perished of disease and never saw combat.

America's most honored national cemetery was born as of one of history's strangest acts of revenge. Credit: U.S. Army photos by Rachel Larue/ Arlington National Cemetery

in person, something that Lee obviously could not do. She actually tried to send a relative with the cash, but the government refused him and ultimately gained control of the estate at the resulting tax auction.

At this point, Union Quartermaster General Montgomery Meigs enters the story. Once described by his own mother as "high tempered, unyielding," and "tyrannical," Meigs was a man defined by great determination, staunch ability, and an abiding bitterness toward Confederates, whom he considered murderous turncoats, an opinion that the loss of his own son in the war had done little to improve. In particular, he felt Robert E. Lee should be among those executed for treason.

So, when the mounting casualties of the war necessitated a new burial ground, Meigs knew precisely

Quiet contemplation of sacrifice is the rule of the day at Arlington National Cemetery, where those who gave all now lie at rest. Credit: U.S. Army photos by Rachel Larue/ Arlington National Cemetery

where to put it. If he could not see Lee killed, he could at least make his foe's home a national graveyard.

Meigs even insisted that bodies be buried closer to the mansion to make it uninhabitable, and specifically interred the remains of more than 2,000 unknown dead directly in Mary Lee's beloved rose garden. When she surveyed the site later, Mrs. Lee wrote with disgust that the graves were "planted up to the very door without any regard to common decency."

As the fighting ended on the battlefield, it began in the courts, with the Lee family trying desperately to stop the burials and regain their land. The legal war would outlive both of them but—by the 1880s—their son would eventually win the day with a 5-4 Supreme Court ruling finding the original tax sale to be illegal. He now held title to his mother's old estate—which was—by this point—filled with about 20,000 graves. He quickly sold it back to the government for a fair price.

A contrived $92 tax bill lost Mary Lee her home, but her heirs were eventually compensated. Credit: U.S. Army photos by Rachel Larue/Arlington National Cemetery

In the end, Arlington stayed, Meigs finally got his way, and in 1892 the former quartermaster was buried in the cemetery he'd worked so hard to create in his enemy's front yard.

However it came to be, no one can deny what it means today. Arlington is now home forever to those who gave their final measure in the nation's defense, and its curious history forever a cherished part of Secret America.

LIFE AFTER LUGGAGE

Where can you find bargains buying items from other people's lost suitcases?

Anyone who has been to an airport has to have a pang of sympathy for it.

There is always that last, forlorn bag on the carousel, doomed to circle endlessly with no one to claim it after all its cousins are snapped up by people getting on with life.

Most of these bags do find their homes. Despite what some flyers might think, only about one in two hundred bags gets lost, and even the vast majority of those are reunited with the person who packed them. Only a tiny fraction are permanently left in limbo, but with nearly 90,000 flights traversing American skies daily, those misplaced totes can add up.

That's where the Unclaimed Baggage Center comes in. Through a partnership with the airlines, many of those bags end up at this facility in Scottsboro, a small town in Alabama hugging the Tennessee River, where their contents are ready to find new lives with bargain hunters.

And buyers are plenty eager. The Huffington Post identifies the center as "one of the top tourist destinations in the state of Alabama," with nearly a million people marching through the doors annually in search of cameras, collectibles, and clothing.

Odder things pop up as well, from suits of armor to human ashes to vacuum-packed frogs. There was a missile guidance system for a fighter jet—which, no doubt, the Air Force was happy to get back, and even a live

About seven thousand new items hit the shelves at the Unclaimed Baggage Center every day.

The end of the line for lost luggage represents a new beginning for the orphaned property of America's air travelers. Credit: Courtesy Unclaimed Baggage Center

rattlesnake—which was not sold.

Such items—along with the innovative nature of the center have made this enterprising part of Secret America a magnet for media attention, getting coverage everywhere from NPR to *The Today Show*. It even made Oprah Winfrey's program in 1995.

There's also a tradition of letting one lucky customer help unpack a mystery bag— prescreened for rattlesnakes or other dangerous items— each day at 2:30 p.m. in what the center dubs "the baggage experience."

Of course, for the 150 or so employees who actually work at the center, the baggage experience is no novelty. It is a large and well-organized operation. The enterprise was named Alabama Retailer of the Year in 2016. That's not bad for an outfit that originally started in 1970 with a $300 loan and some unclaimed bus luggage.

Obviously, all the things found in luggage don't end up being particularly marketable. No one wants your used toothbrushes or half-eaten cupcakes. What can be saved is cleaned and put up for purchase. The rest either sees the trash bin or is donated to charitable concerns. So there may yet be hope for that last bag on the carousel. In Secret America, someone is always going bargain hunting.

UNCLAIMED BAGGAGE CENTER

WHAT The Land of Lost Luggage

WHERE 509 W Willow, Scottsboro, AL

COST Depends on what you find

PRO TIP The center is closed on Sundays.

THE CENTER OF ATTENTION

Why did 600 million IP addresses all end up attached to a single Kansas farmhouse?

With less than 500 people in the 2010 Census, Potwin, Kansas certainly wouldn't strike anyone as being in the middle of everything and yet, cartographically speaking, it happens to be reasonably close. The geographic center of the United States of America is near another Kansas town, Lebanon, just a bit south of the Nebraska border.

And that's how 600 million Internet Protocol addresses all wound up pointing to the nondescript front yard of a single home in the Sunflower State.

The story was first broken when Fusion.net started looking into the matter. Until then, neither residents nor renters seemed to have any idea what was going on. What they did know was that those living at the site were mired in a digital Kafkaesque cul-de-sac on the Information Superhighway that left them targeted by a constant stream of people from IRS agents to folks looking for missing teenagers. Victims of identity theft would stop by in search

In mid-2015, media reports noted that the Internet had finally run out of IP addresses under its old IPV4 system and would now require a newer IPV6 system that would have 340 trillion combinations—which should make the world safe for cat videos for a while.

When 600 million IP addresses lead to your backyard, life is bound to get a bit weird.
Credit: Pixabay

of fraudsters. Some visitors were angry. One even left a broken toilet at the driveway and no one knew quite why.

But what was actually going on turned out to be a fascinating, if vaguely terrifying, example of what happens when you get caught in the teeth of Secret America's digital underbelly. It turns out that a major company in Massachusetts maps IP addresses for thousands of clients. But when a location can't be determined, the company's software had a habit of defaulting to a rounded off set of coordinates for the geographic center of the nation.

But Fusion found other unrelated cases in a similar situation. An Atlanta couple had people showing up looking for stolen mobile devices because of a glitch with an app designed to locate phones. An Ashburn, Virginia man whose proximity to data centers made his home a digital eddy in the great data river had law enforcement show up with a search warrant for a missing government laptop.

Consider that the next time you want to be in the middle of it all.

13 HEADWEAR HOOLIGANISM

Did New Yorkers once riot over unfashionable hats?

There is nothing humorous about civil disorder. Still, it is hard to look at certain instances of public unrest without realizing how little excuse human beings need to unleash civic mayhem. Such is the category for the infamous Straw Hat Riots, which engulfed various sections of Manhattan in a bizarre anarchy during the fall of 1922.

The riots were precisely what the name implies—mass public brawling centered on certain citizens' choice of millinery. Much like the ancient mysterious prohibition on wearing white after Labor Day, it was apparently considered poor form in the Roaring Twenties to don a straw hat after the 15th day of September, and some unruly types in the notoriously nasty Five Points area decided to deputize themselves as impromptu fashion police by knocking off the hats of innocent passersby and then destroying them. Of course, some of the hat-wearers fought back, and soon, things took a turn for the truly violent with angry club-wielding crowds battering one another in the street.

"In some cases, mobs of hundreds of boys and young men terrorized whole blocks," read one media account at the time.

Oddly, the rioting actually started on September 13, two days before the end of straw hat season, but mobs are often unreliable with deadlines.

Things got so out of control that the *New York Times* had to call for peace in an article containing the memorable phrase "the inalienable right of a man to wear a straw hat in a snowstorm," which Thomas Jefferson somehow forgot to enumerate with life, liberty, and the pursuit of happiness.

No one was killed during the troubles, though feelings remained raw. Three years after the riots, the President of

COLUMBUS PARK

WHAT A pleasant green space at the center of a strange riot

WHERE Along Mulberry St., New York, NY

COST None, and you can wear whatever hat you like

NOTEWORTHY A man was reported dead two years after the riots in an altercation over a straw hat.

For 1920s New Yorkers, hats were as good a reason as any for violence in the streets. Credit: Pixabay

the United States made the cover of *The New York Times*— by wearing a straw hat on September 18.

Anyway, much of the disorder seemed to emanate from the Mulberry Bend region of town, which was already on its way up from an unpleasant history of impoverished tenements and gang violence. Indeed, compared to the horrors that had been seen decades earlier in the area made so famous by Martin Scorsese's *Gangs of New York*, riots over hats probably seemed of little consequence. Mulberry Bend Park had come to life there in 1897 and is today's Columbus Park in a bustling part of Chinatown.

The year 1857 saw one of the weirder incidents of civil disorder, in which two rival New York City police forces began beating each other at City Hall injuring about 50 in what became known as the Great New York Police Riot.

THE DAY THE SOUTH INVADED VERMONT

How was a Civil War battle fought in the Green Mountain State?

During the American Civil War, St. Albans, Vermont was about as far from the front lines as any American could hope to get. Less than twenty miles from the Canadian border, the little town off I-89 is far closer to Montreal than Manassas.

And yet, in October 1864, this small city would find that the machinations of a band of Confederate rebels was about to bring the war home to them. Known as the St. Albans Raid, it would become one of the strangest incidents of the war and is still regarded today by townsfolk as its northernmost land battle.

It began when eighteen to twenty-two young Confederate veterans headed south from Canada with a bizarre plan to loot banks and possibly burn towns in service of the Southern cause. They certainly had the element of surprise on their side. When Lt. Bennett Young announced his intention to startled residents, many thought he was joking.

"I take possession of this town in the name of the Confederate States of America," he told the group of stunned Vermonters.

He and his cohorts then proceeded to empty the coffers of three local banks of more than $200,000 claimed in the name of their government.

ST. ALBANS

WHAT A spot well north of Gettysburg

WHERE Taylor Park, St. Albans, VT

COST Free

NOTEWORTHY The events in St. Albans were dramatized in the 1954 film "The Raid" featuring such stars as Anne Bancroft and Lee Marvin.

In the fall of 1864, Atlanta fell to the Union, and St. Albans fought the Confederates. Three guesses which of these battles was dramatized in Gone with the Wind. *Credit: City of St. Albans*

Strange formalities were observed during the event. Captive townspeople were made to swear an oath to the Confederate constitution, and at one point a bank employee even tried to inventory the pilfered funds in hopes that the U.S. government would offer compensation if the losses were truly part of the war.

Soon, however, some in town armed themselves and gunfire broke out. More than half the raiders were caught within a day, but $120,000 had disappeared with the others.

Ultimately, only five of the participants were tried by the Canadian authorities who captured them, and the court ruled that it did not have jurisdiction over what it considered combatant action in a war, so the men got off. In a twist of irony, one of the bank robbers eventually relocated to Texas—where he opened a bank.

The Battle of Salineville, Ohio, is also claimed as the northernmost engagement of Confederate forces, since the St. Albans Confederates were not regulars or wearing uniforms.

15 TALKING TREES

Is there a hidden meaning to oddly shaped trees across the United States?

In eastern Tennessee, an unusual tree bends wildly to one side, its trunk running parallel to the ground before rocketing back up at a right angle. In northern Illinois, a stately old arbor features a secondary limb stretching to one side before reversing upward. In Alabama, a double-trunked tree diverges sharply in opposing directions before bending back with two uprights toward the sky looking vaguely like football goal posts.

Anyone on a nature hike has seen a misshapen tree and sometimes been given to wonder at its origin—a lightning strike, a man-made obstacle to growth, a freakish occurrence. But for many of these strangely sculpted elms, oaks, and maples, their formation was likely no accident. Many preservationists contend that the trees were formed that way on purpose by Native American tribes hundreds of years ago as a way of marking trails well before the advent of traffic signage.

Given the unusual shape of the trees, it seems probable that proponents of the theory are correct—especially when dramatic jogs in the trunk jut outward at angles so strongly pronounced that natural phenomena seem inadequate as an explanation. The trees, found commonly from the Upper Midwest to the American Southeast, could have once pointed the direction of trails, delineated boundaries, shown the way to water and resources, or indicated sites of spiritual importance to local tribes. Some are now protected by organizations, designations, or private owners.

However, many remain without any status, and the massive forest clearance that opened up farmland across the eastern United States in the 19th and 20th centuries took a massive toll. What's left of these signs is now mostly

Dennis Downes, author and researcher, stands between two entrance trail marker trees in Iowa. Credit: Dennis Downes/Great Lakes Trail Marker Tree Society of Antioch, Ill.

TRAIL MARKER TREES

WHAT Trunks with a message

WHERE Eastern United States

COST None

PRO TIP Experts say that one way to tell a genuine trail marker tree is if there is a sharp angular bend a few feet up from the ground.

just remnants of something that was once a much more extensive collection of native markers.

Of course, as expert Dennis Downes, author of *Native American Trail Marker Trees: Marking Paths through the Wilderness*, points out, these trees can still be hard to distinguish from naturally misshapen examples. Well-meaning people may think they've discovered a marker tree when, in fact, they've merely found the result of an ice storm or other natural occurrence. This is particularly true with trees that have a shorter lifespan and wouldn't have been old enough to be used by Native Americans. Some bent trees are just bent trees.

But next time you see a tree with a strange tilt or unique shape, it is possible that it may have been an early version of a road sign.

Trail trees are sometimes also called "message trees" or "thong trees."

31 FLAVORS, 365 ELECTORS

Which first couple has a monument to their first kiss?

We've all had first dates we'd rather forget, however, the one with that special person we'll build our life around is a memory that will always be framed in a special part of our heart. Still, it takes a very special kind of couple to have it framed in granite as well.

Such is the case with Barack and Michelle Obama, a pair who became famous both for their blend of casual suaveness and unpretentious charm and for their genuine romantic chemistry that seemed to light up any room. Not since the Kennedys had the nation seemed so taken with such a young and energetic first family.

It was a measure of that captivation that inspired a Chicago shopping center to erect a 3,000-pound stone monument to the opening chapter of their storybook romance, which began with an excursion on the city's Southside.

"On our first date, I treated her to the finest ice cream Baskin-Robbins had to offer, our dinner table doubling as the curb," recalled the former president in 2007. "I kissed her, and it tasted like chocolate."

The Obama administration may now be a thing of the past, and the Baskin-Robbins may have evolved into a sub sandwich shop, but that didn't stop the shopping center's owner from having the ex-commander-in-chief's words immortalized on a plaque beneath a picture of the couple in

---

The Obamas were married in 1992.

"On our first date, I treated her to the finest ice cream Baskin-Robbins had to offer, our dinner table doubling as the curb. I kissed her, and it tasted like chocolate."

FROM AN INTERVIEW IN O, THE OPRAH MAGAZINE, FEB. 2007.
IMAGE COURTESY OF BLACKPAST.ORG

On this site, President Barack Obama first kissed Michelle Obama.

Wouldn't it be nice if every successful couple's first kiss had its own historical marker? Well, for at least one notable pair, that vision is a reality. Credit: Shutterstock

THE OBAMA KISS MEMORIAL

WHAT A presidential first smooch

WHERE Dorchester Ave. and 53rd St., Chicago, IL

COST None

NOTEWORTHY *Southside with You* earned a 91 percent fresh rating with critics on Rotten Tomatoes.

hopes that the property could hold on to this bit of offbeat presidential history.

In fact, the future first couple's dating itinerary was considered so fascinating that it even inspired a movie in 2016. *Southside with You* is a dramatization of the Obamas' exploits that fateful day, which reportedly included not just ice cream but also a showing of Spike Lee's *Do the Right Thing*.

"Of course, there wasn't a note taker on the dates so you just have to extrapolate from what's there," writer/director Richard Tanne told *Vanity Fair,* noting that he used various sources of public information to reconstruct events. "The trajectory of the date is about 90 percent accurate."

Interestingly, the date isn't the only bit of routine Obama life on display in the Windy City. Not far from the kiss marker is the Hyde Park Hair Salon, a regular haunt for the future president when he needed a trim. But don't think that you can just plop down in the commander-in-chief's seat and ask for a little off the top. Obama's chair is displayed within a glass case complete with the prez's signature.

THE BATTLE OF LOS ANGELES

What exactly attacked America's biggest West Coast city during WWII?

A fleet of Japanese planes? A UFO probe? Assault by an armada of balloons? The so-called Battle of Los Angeles has long remained among the weirdest incidents of WWII. The only thing everyone seems to agree on is that during the overnight hours on the evening of February 24, 1942, all living hell broke loose in the skies over Los Angeles and no one—even three-quarters of a century later—can say for sure exactly why.

Things began when radar began to pick up blips off the coast. Reports of sightings then began to pour in.

But sightings of what exactly? As *The Army Air Forces in World War II* reported: "The next three hours produced some of the most imaginative reporting of the war: 'swarms' of planes (or, sometimes, balloons) of all possible sizes, numbering from one to several hundred, traveling at altitudes which ranged from a few thousand feet to more than twenty thousand and flying at speeds which were said to have varied from 'very slow' to over two hundred miles per hour, were observed to parade across the skies."

Worse, none of whatever it was seemed affected by any of the fourteen hundred or so anti-aircraft shells lobbed in its direction.

The 1979 comedy *1941* was partly inspired by—and an effort to make fun of—the events and the hysteria surrounding the "Battle of Los Angeles."

The Fort MacArthur Museum hosts an event every year to mark the fateful evening that one of America's largest cities never came under attack. Credit: Courtesy of the Fort MacArthur Museum Association

THE FORT MACARTHUR MUSEUM

WHAT A massive air raid (or possibly a weather balloon)

WHERE 3601 S Gaffey St., San Pedro, CA

COST Inquire with the museum

NOTEWORTHY On December 9, 1941, U.S. aircraft were sent to investigate a report of a large Japanese armada of 34 vessels lying in wait off the coast for an attack on Los Angeles, only to find that the supposed invasion fleet turned out to consist of American fishing boats.

As to what caused all of it when the smoke cleared the next day, the U.S. military couldn't even agree with itself. The Navy said it was just a false alarm while the Army insisted that some kind of aircraft had buzzed the city. The War Department concluded that planes were launched from Japanese subs or airfields in Mexico. For their part, the post-war Japanese government said they never raided Los Angeles and have no idea what happened.

After extensive investigation, many have settled on that most cliched of explanations for unexplained goings-on in the night sky—a weather balloon. One or more such balloons may indeed have set off the alert, and then a combination of public panic and nervous trigger fingers may have done the rest.

The Fort MacArthur Museum in the Los Angeles area still holds commemorative events each February to keep the memory of the incident alive.

A HAIRY HISTORY

How did a billing dispute over a wig cause the Boston Massacre?

If there is anything Americans love more than cutting history class, it is romanticizing what little history we actually bothered to learn. Perhaps nowhere is this more apparent than in our recollection of the Boston Massacre, a March 1770 event that is still recalled fondly as a sort of Massachusetts version of the Alamo, with martyred patriots standing up to speak truth to power. The reality, of course, is much different.

The Boston Massacre was mostly started by a fight over a wigmaker's invoice.

In fact, virtually everything you know about this seminal event of Colonial rebellion is probably wrong. There wasn't much patriotism involved—just nervous soldiers, a hostile, possibly drunken, crowd, and a chaotically tragic ending to a remarkably mundane argument.

It all began with a British officer by the name of John Goldfinch, who was alleged to have an outstanding debt to a local wigmaker, whose apprentice, Edward Gerrish, was unhappily heckling the fellow about it. Nearby, a British private named Hugh White noticed the developing dispute, and after a brief and unpleasant conversation and possibly some shoving, decided to end the argument with a musket

---

The famous "one if by land, two if by sea" lanterns were never meant to warn Paul Revere of British movements but were actually arranged by Revere to warn his allies if he could not make it out of Boston.

The infamous Redcoats may not have been the brutes they were portrayed to be during the Boston Massacre. Credit: Pixabay

THE BOSTON MASSACRE SITE

WHAT Musket smoke and sentimental inaccuracies

WHERE The intersection of Devonshire and State Sts., Boston, MA

COST Your illusions from civics class

NOTEWORTHY The famous Boston Tea Party wasn't called the Boston Tea Party until at least 1826—a full five decades after it happened.

butt delivered sharply to Gerrish's cranium.

But the apprentice's headache didn't deter him, and soon he returned with a mob. Reinforcements arrived to disperse the unruly crowd, which responded by pelting the guards with snowballs and screaming at them to open fire, which—in the tension and confusion—someone did. That shot caused others to discharge their weapons without orders.

After the shots, five lay dead in a sad testament to mixing ill-trained, jumpy soldiers with an angry mob. Other embellishments about the affair came courtesy of propagandists pumping venom into the public bloodstream with fantastic depictions of innocent protesters being brutally slaughtered by murderous Redcoats run amok.

Notably, Founding Father John Adams, later to become our second president, defended the Brits in court—and actually managed to get most of them acquitted. Today, the site of the famous shooting is still marked. A stone disc girdled with stars is inlaid upon the pavement at the site.

THE MISSING LETTER ON TESTS

Why is there no "E" on the grading scale?

As any child who failed to study before an exam can attest, many of us grew to hate the sixth character of the alphabet from an early age. There was no greater ignominy than taking home a paper emblazoned with a giant red "F"—that most shameful of scarlet letters.

Yet, the A–F system has had a certain staying power one has to admire. It remains the default for countless classes, due mainly to its simplicity. But whether you wish to worship it or curse it, you can actually visit its birthplace right here in America. Welcome to Mount Holyoke College in South Hadley, Massachusetts, where they didn't invent the report card, but in 1897 they did invent the grades you probably saw on yours.

Previous to that, students were often grouped by numbers, Roman numerals, or some other rating system. The late 18th century actually saw Yale grade a paper with the

MOUNT HOLYOKE COLLEGE

WHAT Where your report card began

WHERE 50 College St., South Hadley, MA

COST $62,000 (tuition plus room and board and student activity fees) as of 2017–2018

NOTEWORTHY Mount Holyoke's nearly 2,200 students come from seventy-four different nations.

Mount Holyoke was the first of the "Seven Sisters" colleges that garnered that name by catering to women.

Mount Holyoke College in South Hadley, Massachusetts, is where the alphabet soup of the modern grading system began. Credit: Courtesy Mount Holyoke College

poetic-sounding label "optimi" for best. Lesser students got the rather uncreatively named "second optimi," while lower grades earned you an "inferiore" or "pejores."

In 1883, Harvard doled out a "B" to a student. But the move to a true letter-based system came from Mount Holyoke, though the school, founded in 1837, didn't actually adopt the current A–F grading. In fact, it had the more alphabetically satisfying A–E. It should also be noted that the scale would have made even good students beg for a curve. The lowest grade of E was for anything below 75 percent—which is now a middle "C" in most places. Grades as high as 94 percent only earned you a "B." The migration from "E" to "F" was because "fail" started with "F". Hence "E" was banished from gradebooks.

Pressures in modern education have pushed in the other direction, however. During Vietnam, when a poor grade could kill a draft deferment, some profs began protecting students with higher marks. This trend later reappeared due to fiscal pressure on schools. A 2012 study at Yale found that sixty-two percent of grades were "A," leading *USA Today* to ask in a headline whether "A" now stood for "average".

20

GEM OF THE MOUNTAIN

Was the state of Idaho named for a hoax?

Reflecting the nation's diverse cultural heritage, the names of the states come from an array of different sources. Some, like Delaware or Pennsylvania, are namesakes of people. Others, like Virginia or New York show the country's British heritage, while numerous Western states, such as Nevada or Montana, are derived from Spanish. Louisiana and Vermont remind us of our connections to France.

Yet what of Idaho? The answer is that no one really knows, but the story may indicate one of the funniest hoaxes ever put over on the American public.

The story begins just before the Civil War when westward expansion was bringing new territories and states into the Union at a rapid clip and there were often battles in Congress over naming issues, with Spanish and Native American words being popular choices. Yet, many of these names were surprisingly arbitrary. Chosen for how they sounded, they might not always be directly connected to a particular region. Idaho, said to be an Indian word meaning "gem of the mountain," fell into this category. Initially, it was chosen for what we today call Colorado.

But before the Rocky Mountain State could be tagged with the moniker, backers discovered the whole thing was something of a fraud. No one can say precisely where the word "Idaho" came from, although virtually everyone now agrees that it wasn't from any Indian language. The prime suspect in the matter is a fellow by the name of George Willing, a local politico who appears to have simply made the entire thing up out of whole cloth and then given it fictional Native American origins.

According to one of Willing's friends, he seemed to get a kick out of his fabricated insertion into American linguistics

The name may not translate to one, but Idaho is forever a gem to those who live there. Credit: Pixabay

and had invented "Idaho"—often rendered "E dah hoe"—with "the most gleeful appreciation of the humor of the thing."

In later years, various mythologies popped up about Idaho's origin, prompting research as to which Indian language it hailed from. The answer turned out to be none of them. Idaho's exact etymology—if it actually has one—is probably lost to history. It could indeed be no more than a random assortment of syllables thought to sound catchy.

The origin for the name of neighboring Oregon is mostly unknown, with a wide assortment of theories ranging from the spice oregano to a region of Spain named Aragon.

21

EMINENT DISTAIN

What does this strange mosaic on a New York sidewalk mean?

Few arguments can provoke quite as much emotion as a good old-fashioned land dispute. Something about the American fascination with owning property always seems to get the blood boiling when real estate is at stake. Moreover, the wounds and resulting grudges can last well beyond resolution of the original matter. Perhaps nowhere on Earth is this better illustrated than at the corner of Seventh Avenue and Christopher Street in New York City, where a tiny triangular message embedded in the sidewalk sits in mute testament to one family's attempt to fight the powers-that-be.

"PROPERTY OF THE HESS ESTATE," it reads boldly in all caps, "WHICH HAS NEVER BEEN DEDICATED FOR PUBLIC PURPOSES."

What on Earth does that mean?

Without knowing the background, this odd pronouncement could certainly leave the uninitiated scratching their heads. But the story is well worth a little research. The strange roots of what became known as the Hess Triangle dates to the early days of the 20th century when apartments owned by local resident David Hess were targeted for a buyout due to street work for a new subway line. Hess was distinctly unhappy to see his building meet its demise and tried to prevent the authorities from taking it. Unfortunately, eminent domain is a cruel mistress, and the march of progress ultimately allowed the government to purchase the land whether Hess liked it or not.

This spot is also sometimes known as the Spite Triangle.

THE HESS TRIANGLE

WHAT An isosceles icon to indomitable ire

WHERE Seventh Ave. and Christopher St., New York City, NY

COST None

PRO TIP The Stonewall National Monument celebrating the gay rights movement is just a block to the east of the Hess site.

This three-sided statement of pique may no longer be property of the Hess Estate, but it remains a thing of beauty to anyone who has ever lost a battle against city hall. Credit: Jason Eppink via Flickr under Creative Commons 2.0

But while Hess might not have been able to fight city hall, he could at least give it a black eye. It turned out that a surveying oversight left a tiny tricornered scrap of property outside the buyout. When the issue was discovered, the authorities asked that the few hundred square inches be given to the city.

The Hess family had a better plan for it. Measuring just over two feet on each side, the triangle was inlaid with tile and transformed into a marker for Hess's anger. For a time, it was thought to be among the smallest chunks of privately owned real estate in the city, perhaps the whole nation.

Created in 1922, it was sold just before the Second World War for $1,000 to what is now Village Cigars, where it remains to this day just outside the front door—a defiant piece of private land the government never did get its hands on. The city may have gotten its subway line, but Hess got the last laugh.

22

MAINE DUNES

How did a desert end up in America's northeasternmost state?

Maine is a more diverse state than many give it credit for. Largely known for lighthouses and lobsters, it also has some really beautiful beaches and some of the most impressive forests this side of a Tolkien book.

But near Freeport, you'll find the one thing you'd swear you wouldn't run into within this land of coastline and conifers. Desert Road off I-295 isn't just a bit of imaginative nomenclature.

The Desert of Maine has been a fun destination in the area since the 1920s, when a creative fellow snapped up the seemingly worthless land for $300 in hopes of creating a unique tourist attraction out of its sandy dunes. The Saharan environment doesn't extend far. The whole place is around forty acres, but the proprietors make the most of it, offering tours, sand designing, nature trails, gemstone hunts, and a gift shop, as well as a museum in an 18th century barn.

And just what exactly is a barn doing in the middle of a desert? That's a clue to the origins of this unusual site. It was once a farm—in fact, quite a fertile one. But the Tuttle family who worked the land failed to steward it properly. Overgrazing and lack of crop rotation began to destroy the area's natural top soil. According to Smithsonian.com, the desert began as "a patch of silt the size of a dinner plate." Unfortunately for the Tuttles, it didn't stay that way. The

THE DESERT OF MAINE

WHAT A dustbowl among the evergreens

WHERE 95 Desert Rd., Freeport, ME

COST $6.75–$12.50 depending on age

PRO TIP You can fill your own sand bottles at the desert as souvenirs for an extra charge

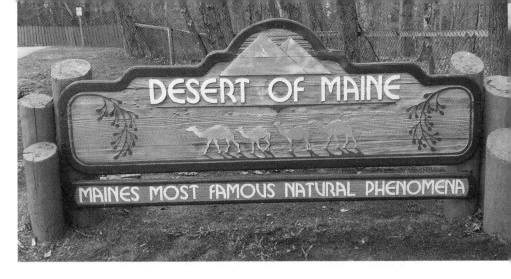

There are bigger deserts than this one, but none are as convenient to the Eastern Seaboard. Credit: Desert of Maine

sand became an unstoppable force that killed all chances of continued agriculture.

The idea of desertification isn't science fiction. As Smithsonian points out, much the same thing happened to farmers in Oklahoma during the Depression-era Dust Bowl. Treat nature with cavalier disregard and she might exact her revenge.

But while the desert may have been exposed by man, it isn't man-made. The Tuttles' farming practices were merely uncovering an ancient and fascinating part of Maine's geological history, when roaming glaciers crushed rock into the dunes we see today. The sand is quite real and naturally deposited. Of course, the desert's rainfall levels are the same as the rest of the area, so don't expect arid expanses under a pitiless sun, but the dunes aren't artificial. There was always a desert here under the once-lush fields.

Whoever said geology couldn't be interesting?

The sand in the Desert of Maine
is called glacial silt.

23 THE SECRET BEHIND LINCOLN'S HEAD

What is housed in a hidden, inaccessible room atop Mt. Rushmore?

Even Americans who haven't had the pleasure of a visit to South Dakota have probably seen enough photos of its most famous landmark that they can picture it in their sleep—four noble faces etched in timeless rock memorializing presidents who were themselves larger than life.

But there is a part of this monument that that postcard picture in your mind doesn't show. Nestled above the sculptures and hidden behind Honest Abe's likeness is a strange doorway leading to a mysterious seventy-five-foot long chamber with a sealed titanium enclosure. Yes, believe it or not, there is a secret room with a private vault behind Abraham Lincoln's head.

The reason for its existence dates back to sculptor Gutzon Borglum. While the government was interested in budgets and timelines, Borglum was thinking bigger.

Incensed at what it felt was Alfred Hitchcock's violation of the terms of his agreement to depict no violent scenes while filming at Mt. Rushmore for 1959's *North by Northwest*, the National Park Service asked that it be removed from the credits of the iconic film, calling the site's use a "desecration."

Abe may be honest, but his head hides a secret he isn't sharing with the other presidents. Credit: David Baugher

MT. RUSHMORE

WHAT A room with no view

WHERE Mt. Rushmore, SD

COST None. The secret room cannot be visited or seen

NOTEWORTHY The mountain is named for Charles Rushmore, a New York attorney who happened to be in the area on business in the 1880s. According to various sources, his surname became attached to the site when he asked its name. He was told it didn't have one and his guide joked they should just start calling it "Rushmore."

He was preoccupied by what future archeologists might make of these weathered stone visages centuries or perhaps millennia after the United States itself might lay forgotten. He didn't want his grand achievement to simply become an obscure curiosity for posterity to puzzle over.

The solution Borglum conceived was a "Hall of Records" that would tell any future folk what all this grandiose face-carving had been about. There would be tablets, documents, busts, and even a massive gold-plated eagle.

However, though work was begun, it was never finished, and the stone entryway was all that remained when more than a dozen years of construction wrapped up in 1941.

In 1998, pleas by Borglum's descendants and funding by the Mount Rushmore National Memorial Society allowed tablets explaining the sculpture and copies of documents to be placed near the doorway to the special room, which tourists cannot visit due to its inaccessible location.

But at least now you know it is there.

24 THE AMAZING CLOSET OF DARYL DAVIS

Why does an African American blues musician own dozens of Ku Klux Klan robes, and what lesson might the country learn from his story?

Daryl Davis is a talented blues musician who has played with some of the greats, from Jerry Lee Lewis to Chuck Berry. Yet it is the contents of his closet that might amaze most people. It contains about three dozen or so Ku Klux Klan robes.

But these clothes didn't belong to Davis. In fact, Davis wouldn't even be eligible for KKK membership.

That's because Daryl Davis is black.

The stunning story of how Davis acquired the robes—and what his incredible closet might teach our divided nation about the simple power of civility—dates back to the early 1980s when he struck up a conversation with a white audience member after playing a gig at a lounge. After complimenting Davis's skillful piano playing, the fellow eventually revealed to Davis that he was part of the local KKK.

DARYL DAVIS'S CLOSET

WHAT The most amazing closet in Secret America

WHERE Not open to the public, but Davis hopes someday to open a museum to display his robe collection

COST Not applicable

PRO TIP Davis said that looking for commonalities is key to communication, noting that you can find something in common even with your worst enemy. "As we focus more and more, and find more things in common, things we have in contrast, such as skin color, matter less and less," he told one interviewer.

Daryl Davis holds up a Ku Klux Klan robe, one of many he possesses from former members who became convinced to leave after he made friends with them. Credit: Courtesy Daryl Davis

For most people, that would have been the end of the discussion. But Davis isn't most people. He continued to converse—and even struck up a friendship with his new acquaintance. He used that connection to meet more people in the Klan and made friends with some of them.

"How can you hate me if you don't even know me?" he would ask those reluctant to engage him.

Upon talking to him, some did indeed befriend him—and many of them eventually gave up their membership in the organization. They found it impossible to be racist against African Americans when they were friends with one.

The Southern Poverty Law Center estimates that there are about 5,000 to 8,000 Klansmen in the United States.

Davis's quest to promote understanding has led him to places many might fear to tread. Credit: Courtesy Daryl Davis

Davis didn't debate or nag or yell or moralize. Instead he built relationships and had respectful conversations— listening as well as talking. He made comrades of those who should have been his enemies. He shared his perspective and allowed others to share their own—no matter how offensive he found their views to be. In effect, he converted people by not trying to convert them.

And with each man who finally left the Klan under the power of Davis's polite persuasion, the musician collected yet another robe. As his clothing collection grew, the Klan shrank. Even prominent members of the KKK are not immune. Davis's first meeting with one high official in the group was so tense that the white man brought an armed bodyguard who kept his hand near his weapon.

Today, the man's robe is in Davis's collection. The former Klansman eventually asked the musician to be godfather to his daughter.

Davis's mind-blowing story was chronicled in his book, *Klan-destine Relationships: A Black Man's Odyssey in the Ku Klux Klan,* and a more recent movie *Accidental Courtesy: Daryl Davis, Race & America.* He continues to befriend Klansmen to this day and continues—in some instances—to see them leave the Klan with their former KKK clothing joining his closet, yet another example of how dialogue can triumph where disputatiousness fails. It's a lesson we all might take to heart in an era where public discourse has become so venomous and toxic.

Of course, Davis's unusual friendships have provoked controversy as well. Some racial and social justice advocates have been unhappy with his non-confrontational approach.

Davis's response is simple. In an interview with *The Atlantic,* he posed a question for those critical of what he has accomplished.

"How many robes and hoods have you collected?" he asked.

25

THE MANY FACETS OF FASCES

Why does the Lincoln Memorial have fascist symbols on it?

Abraham Lincoln probably ranks among our most beloved presidents. Indeed, historians often put the man from the five-dollar bill as among our very best commanders-in-chief due to the fortitude with which he faced the nation's most harrowing moments. Not bad for a young lawyer from Springfield.

But if you look closely at the memorial to this great man, you'll find something unexpected. Beneath Lincoln's resting arms are carvings of bundled reeds. These reeds have a particular political meaning. They are called fasces and are prominent symbols of the ideology known as fascism, made famous by Italian strongman Benito Mussolini.

This isn't a joke or a conspiracy theory. Nor is the Lincoln Monument alone in hosting these insignia. They figure into the design at the Department of Justice, the House of Representatives, the Supreme Court Building, even the Oval Office itself. Even the dime had a fasces on its reverse through the early 20th century. So what's going on here?

First, it is important to understand that fascists didn't invent the fasces. The bundle of reeds, often with an ax blade at its head, dates back to Roman times as a symbol of

---

The swastika is yet another symbol that went from innocuous to infamous thanks to fascism. Before Hitler, it was an ancient symbol whose name meant "good fortune" or "well-being."

IN THIS TEMPLE
AS IN THE HEARTS OF THE PEOPLE
FOR WHOM HE SAVED THE UNION
THE MEMORY OF ABRAHAM LINCOLN
IS ENSHRI..D FOREVER

See those bundled reeds under Lincoln's arms? Yep. Those are called fasces, the symbol from which the ideology of fascism takes its name. Credit: Pixabay

THE LINCOLN MEMORIAL

WHAT Honest Abe's armrests

WHERE Washington, DC

COST Free

NOTEWORTHY House Speaker Joe Cannon, a huge fan of Lincoln, fought very hard AGAINST the memorial honoring his hero because he didn't like the plan to overhaul the Washington Mall.

power. Fascism was enamored of the idea of people bonding together—under the state—to find strength in numbers. Reeds tied together—as in a fasces—cannot be broken as they might individually. Like other classical symbols of power, this one also made it into designs for American edifices connoting ideas of durability and unity.

Still, the associations aren't entirely innocent. Prior to World War II, many major American thinkers were actually surprisingly amicable with Mussolini. Even that most American of Americans, Will Rogers, said he was "pretty high" on the Italian tyrant, and Franklin Delano Roosevelt said he was "deeply impressed" by the accomplishments of "that admirable Italian gentleman." People, including those who had the power to design public works, weren't necessarily anti-fascist until war clouds began to gather.

But don't worry. You needn't toss out your five-dollar bills. The fasces spread across Washington simply show that the symbolism of politics can have tangled roots indeed.

26

A NIGHT AT THE MUSEUM

Where can you climb through a playground made of steel, slides, and imagination?

Let's face it. If you hear the words "city museum," you probably aren't that enthused for a visit. It sounds like the kind of place that kids end up on a field trip where the best part is getting out of school for a day.

But that's only if you don't live in St. Louis, Missouri, where those two words connote a night out that even adults will love.

After all, what kind of museum has an old bus perched off the edge of its roof, boasts enchanted caves, and allows you to clamber through an airplane fuselage a couple stories off the ground? And very few museums advise you to bring a flashlight, wear sneakers, or buy kneepads at the gift shop.

As Whet Moser of *Chicago* magazine puts it, City Museum "is like something conceived by a child with an arc welder and access to an unlimited amount of scrap metal." Actually, this quirky spot housed in a former shoe factory was conceived by the late Bob Cassilly, an artist, sculptor, and all-around creator who brought this place to life as a bizarre mixture of walking, climbing, sliding, and generally traversing a multi-floor maze of "exhibits" that appear to have been constructed entirely from items found around a recycled materials center. Its 600,000 square feet contain all manner of discarded equipment, repurposed glass, stone, shells, and pretty much anything else that can be made into an interactive experience.

CITY MUSEUM

WHAT A museum like no other

WHERE 750 N 16th St., St. Louis, MO

COST $12 for ages three and up/ $10 Friday and Saturday after 5 p.m.

PRO TIP There may be lines if you arrive in the morning.

If you are expecting stuffy art collections and quiet contemplation of historical or aesthetic significance, St. Louis's City Museum will come as quite a surprise. Credit: Courtesy City Museum

There are also water features, a rooftop cantina, a human-sized hamster wheel, a shoelace factory, a pipe organ and an entire log cabin. There is even an artificial cave system inside the building in which to get lost.

Oh, yes, and don't forget the slides which seem to be everywhere you look—including a ten-story spiral one.

In case you are still bored, you can take a look at the world's largest pencil, a seventy-six-foot long, 22,000 lbs. writing implement. (It's a No. 2, of course). The eraser alone weighs 250 pounds. The "puking pig" is another centerpiece at the institution. It's an old boiler fitted with a pig-shaped face that fills with water and tips periodically to disgorge its contents. The entire outdoor structure is a multi-story jungle gym/art project known as the MonstroCity. The remains of two former airplanes are lodged here within an interconnected network of twisted metal.

Though it isn't well-known nationally, City Museum is locally beloved and is an ever-popular option for everything from family nights out to creative first dates.

Best of all, the facility is an ever-changing experience. The slogan at City Museum is "Always Building".

City Museum opened in 1997.

27

WHEN CONNECTICUT OWNED OHIO

Why is Case Western Reserve University named that?

Case Western Reserve University has long had a grand academic reputation and regularly appears in rankings of top schools around the nation.

Yet the name of the institution might sound a bit odd to the uninitiated. "Case" could be correctly assumed to be the name of a person—in this instance Leonard Case Jr., an initial funder of the school. Yet, what precisely is a "Western Reserve" University? Reserved by whom? And for what?

The answer lies in the twisted roots of a much larger story about the nation's early days, when states held vague and frequently contradictory claims to large tracts of western lands.

Massachusetts held claims to parts of New York, Michigan, and Wisconsin. Georgia insisted that it owned most of what is today Alabama and Mississippi. South Carolina believed itself the rightful heir to a ludicrously narrow strip that ran all the way to the Mississippi. New York felt it had title to massive stretches of the Ohio River Valley. Virginia may have maintained the biggest claims, encompassing an area from

CASE WESTERN RESERVE UNIVERSITY

WHAT Connecticut on the Cuyahoga

WHERE 10900 Euclid Ave., Cleveland, OH

COST $22,796 per semester for 12 credit hours or more

NOTEWORTHY The last state to cede its western lands was Georgia, which did so in 1802.

Cleveland is allegedly the result of a map misspelling of Moses Cleaveland's name.

Left: The very name of this campus reflects northern Ohio's linkage to a distant state it doesn't even border. Credit: Case Western Reserve University

Kentucky to Minnesota. These claims were sometimes predicated on royal grants dating to the Colonial era, when maps were based less on reliable cartography and more on vague guesses referencing geographic features that were either misplaced, distorted, or mythical. It wasn't unusual for areas to be claimed by as many as three states at the same time.

Most of these disputes were eventually resolved with cessions to the federal government, and Connecticut, which claimed chunks of real estate going all the way out to present-day Chicago, generally gave up its lands as well. But it did insist on keeping more than three million acres abutting Pennsylvania in what is now northeastern Ohio, known as the "Connecticut Western Reserve," which ended up being settled by a fair number of Connecticutians. Incidentally, Cleveland is actually named after Moses Cleaveland, a Connecticut native who founded the city and then showed his love for the place by returning immediately to Connecticut and never coming back.

Anyway, by 1800, even Connecticut had ceded its excess back to the federal government. But its stubbornness in hanging onto a "western reserve" nearly 500 miles from its borders is still reflected in the name of one of the nation's finest universities.

28

IOWA—THE FINAL FRONTIER

Where is Captain Kirk's hometown?

Sometimes it seems like no town is too small to have at least one local boy who made good, a notable resident who ends up featured on the city limit sign with a "Home of . . ." introduction. Of course, it always feels a bit hollow. Mr. Important has long since departed the area for New York, Los Angeles, or more suitable surroundings in which to be famous.

But smack dab between Davenport and Des Moines, the tiny berg of Riverside, Iowa, can brag that its most famous resident hasn't left town. In fact, he hasn't even arrived yet. Captain James T. Kirk won't be born here until 2228. The future captain of the *Enterprise* is due to arrive on March 22, in case you'd like to mark your interstellar calendars. No word on what stardate that might be. Still, the date may be in some dispute. Startrek.com puts it as 2233, so perhaps Kirk was fudging his age on his academy application form. After all, he did cheat on the Kobayashi Maru test. I guess we'll know in about two centuries.

In case you are wondering, this is all completely "canon," as the Trekkies like to call it. Kirk mentioned his birthplace as Iowa in the fourth *Star Trek* film in 1986, but failed to note a specific hometown. That's how the enterprising folks of Riverside decided to have the town council declare that their particular corner of eastern Iowa is the intrepid explorer's

---

Riverside is 17.8 miles from I-80, the nearest interstate, but 4.37 light years from Proxima Centauri, the nearest star system.

Riverside's favorite son is due to make his appearance just over two centuries from now, so you still have time to get something nice for the baby shower.
Credit: Peter Zillmann via Flickr under Creative Commons 2.0

CAPTAIN KIRK'S BIRTHPLACE

WHAT The center of the Star Trek universe

WHERE Riverside, Iowa, Terran System, Milky Way Galaxy

COST The Federation doesn't use money

PRO TIP Check out trekfest. org for details on upcoming events.

birthplace. The proactive decision to sponsor Kirk's birth was eventually ratified by an even higher authority—none other than the late Gene Roddenberry himself.

Moreover, the town takes its role plenty seriously. Not only does its sign announce Kirk's birthplace but, according to a *Chicago Tribune* article, a stone pillar even marks the street he will grow up on, while a local tavern has gone further still, putting up a plaque on its wall to show where Kirk will be conceived.

Perhaps "too much information" isn't a 23rd Century concept.

Anyway, Riverside's annual celebration was renamed Trek Fest, which was set to mark its 33rd year in 2017. A museum was opened and there is even a model starship—Constitution class, of course—to honor Kirk. It isn't the *Enterprise*, though. Rather, it is the U.S.S. *Riverside*.

Perhaps most importantly, the locals have taken to raising cash through crowdfunding to put up their very own statue of their most famous soon-to-be resident.

29

PYRAMIDS AND POLITICS

Why did the U.S. government build a half-billion-dollar pyramid and vote to stop funding it the day after it became fully operational?

There are many strange-looking parts of Secret America, but the one protruding from the stark plains of North Dakota may be the most prominent. Then again, a giant pyramid is hard to miss—especially a federally built, flat-topped one that looks very much like the sort seen on the dollar bill. Surrounded by barbed wire-topped fencing, it seems like the sort of thing specially designed to fuel Masonic-style conspiracy theories.

But the real story of why this bizarre structure is here is even stranger than fiction. Welcome to the Stanley R. Mikelsen Safeguard Complex, a high-tech, cutting-edge Defense Department installation that the government spent several years and $486 million to build—and that it abandoned within a matter of weeks.

The reason can be found in that most copious wellspring of irrationality—politics. The complex was the victim of a Cold War debate over policy. It was designed as an anti-ballistic missile facility that would shoot down inbound Russian ICBMs. This wasn't to protect people, but rather to protect other missiles—at least those based in North Dakota—thus giving the United States a chance to counterattack. This theory of mutually assured destruction was supposedly the rationale undergirding the détente between the superpowers so the world wouldn't end.

At the time, the anti-ballistic missile facility project was the largest single contract awarded by the U.S. Army Corps of Engineers.

After consuming nearly half-a-billion dollars of taxpayer money, this giant pyramid was fully operational for exactly one day before the government announced its funding was cut. Credit: Benjamin Halpern, Historic American Engineering Record, via Library of Congress

STANLEY R. MIKELSEN SAFEGUARD COMPLEX

WHAT A pyramid in the middle of nowhere

WHERE It can be viewed from 81st St. just outside Nekoma, ND

COST About as much as anything in the defense budget

PRO TIP This is private property. Do not enter the grounds.

But the world ended for the Mikelsen complex rather quickly. Even during construction in 1970, anti-nuclear protestors showed up to express displeasure, which involved planting a tree of peace at the site as well as, according to at least one eyewitness, a good deal of drugs and free love.

But while hippie sex failed to stop the project, opposition in Congress eventually doomed it. Partially operational in the spring of 1975, it would get a complete complement of missiles on October 1. The very next day, the facility's opponents finally got the upper hand and cut the purse strings, with operations effectively ending the following month. It was decommissioned the next year, leaving behind 27,500 tons of steel, 714,000 cubic feet of concrete, and one of the oddest-looking white elephants in history. Today, the land belongs to a nearby self-sustaining religious community that mainly uses it to grow crops.

Meanwhile, a giant disused pyramid lurks over northeastern North Dakota, courtesy of Cold War fears and the whims of a fickle Congress.

30

THE MAN WITH NO BRAND

Who was the fellow whose name came to define the idea of challenging the status quo, and why are his cows important?

Today, "maverick" may be a part of the English language, but it is very much an American word—one that strikes a deep chord for residents of a nation that prides itself on the value of individuality and being different. It is no accident that the term has immortalized itself through television characters, sports teams, and even a make of car. Conformism is passé. To be a maverick means to be an original.

But if so, who was the original "original"? Who was the very first maverick?

In fact, that honor goes to Samuel Augustus Maverick, a steely Texan who served as a lawyer, legislator, and military commander and eventually became one of the early mayors of San Antonio. You can see his signature today on a copy of the state's Declaration of Independence in the capitol.

But surprisingly, the term "maverick" was less about this man's adventures and more about his lackadaisical attitude toward marking his cattle. The word began because the rancher habitually refused to brand his herd. By some accounts, Maverick found branding to be inhumane, though others suspect his aversion was a ploy

---

The family surname isn't the only contribution the Mavericks have made to the English language. Fontaine Maury Maverick, grandson of Sam, is credited with creating the word "gobbledygook" to describe regulatory prose.

These three things have all been named after someone's unlabeled cows. Left: Credit: Per-Olof Forsberg via Flickr under Creative Commons 2.0 *Middle:* Credit: Greg Gjerdingen via Flickr under Creative Commons 2.0 *Right:* Credit: Derek Bridges via Flickr under Creative Commons 2.0

THE TEXAS DECLARATION OF INDEPENDENCE

WHAT The signature of the original Maverick

WHERE Austin, TX

COST None

NOTEWORTHY Though connected strongly with Texas, Sam Maverick wasn't a native. He was born in South Carolina.

to let the cattleman to pick up any unbranded stray animals he found and claim them as his own.

Whatever the reason, neighbors used the term to mean any cattle who didn't have a brand, and it eventually became regularly applied to the sort of folks who don't run with the herd.

Since then, others have cashed in on the concept. Ford named a vehicle after it, Dallas's basketball team adopted the moniker, and James Garner became famous as Bret Maverick, a sharp-witted card player on the TV series of the same name. GOP nominee John McCain was famous for labeling himself a maverick in 2008, though the Arizona senator's use of the term didn't sit well with some in the Maverick family. During the campaign, Maverick's descendant Terrellita Maverick told *The New York Times* that she was "enraged" at McCain's self-description.

"He's a Republican," she said bluntly. "He's branded."

31

OAKEN OWNERSHIP

Does a tree in Athens, Georgia, really have title to its own land?

Becoming a property owner is true rite of passage. What other milestone in life better expresses the feeling of becoming a master of one's own fate? But in the college town of Athens, Ga., about 70 miles east of Atlanta, there is a decidedly unique deedholder—one that truly is attached to the land.

This city has a tree that owns itself.

"For and in consideration of the great love I bear this tree and the great desire I have for its protection," reads a plaque in front of a stately oak, "for all time, I convey entire possession of itself and all land within eight feet of the tree on all sides."

Yep, you read that right. This tree not only owns itself but even has a bit of a front yard to spread into. The genesis of this odd arrangement stems to the 1800s and a fellow by the name of Colonel William H. Jackson who was enamored enough of a three-and-a-half century-old tree that he decided it deserved its own tract of property. Since then, the tree has really put down roots in the community, with a philanthropist paying to put a protective enclosure around it.

"Its property rights have never been questioned," reads a description on an Athens tourism site.

Unfortunately, while neighbors might respect the tree's home turf, Mother Nature was a tougher sell. Jackson's

THE TREE THAT OWNS ITSELF

WHAT The nation's strangest landholder

WHERE The corner of Dearing and Finely Sts., Athens, GA

COST None

PRO TIP If you visit at Christmas, you'll find the tree fully decorated in its holiday finery.

This tree is one of Athens's most prominent property owners. Credit: Courtesy VisitAthensGA.com

original tree fell victim to a storm during World War II, and a new tree had to be installed thanks to the friendly ministrations of the Junior Ladies Garden Club.

Not that the replacement oak is a stranger. It was grown from one of the acorns of the departed tree, meaning that this tree managed not only to hold property but to convey it to a descendant. That's impressive since the tree—like so many who fail at estate planning—never even left a will.

Anyway, as *Mental Floss* is quick to note, the issue of whether the tree truly owns the land is a legally dubious one. First of all, the actual deed is lost to history and, secondly . . . well, it's a tree. State law doesn't recognize property ownership by plant life.

But legalisms can take a backseat when romantic notions are at stake. As far as the good people of Athens are concerned, this is one tree that holds its own mortgage.

Some have thrown birthday parties for the tree, and its descendants have been planted by local children each Arbor Day.

32

SLEEPING WITH THE FISHES

Where can I find an underwater hotel?

Any veteran traveler knows that the lodging experience all starts to look the same after a while. Soon you feel like every roadside inn is nothing but a blur of single-serving soaps, continental breakfasts, and an ice machine located too far down the hall. But there are places where you can make an overnight stay just as much of an adventure as the destination itself.

Welcome to the Jules' Undersea Lodge in Key Largo, Florida.

This is no gimmick. You can indeed room beneath the waves of a charming lagoon just off U.S. Route 1. The lodge is actually a converted underwater laboratory retrofitted into two bedrooms of submerged comfort 21 feet below the water line.

Notably, the 10,000-plus guests who have made the trip to commune with the Sunshine State's marine life get the true sea lab experience. There are no stairs, no elevator, and no tunnel. You arrive at your undersea suite in full dive gear, emerging via an opening in the floor of the "wet room."

Meanwhile, guests get all the amenities: climate control, communications, and DVD/VCR capability along with power, fresh water, and of course, a continuous supply of air so things don't get stuffy.

JULES' UNDERSEA LODGE

WHAT A suite at sea

WHERE 51 Shoreland Dr., Key Largo, FL

COST Overnight single-person stays are $675 but rates for different packages vary widely

PRO TIP Since there are only two rooms, cancellation policies are quite strict. Consult www.jul.com for details.

Dinner can have a certain flair when it must be delivered via a fellow in scuba gear. Credit: Courtesy Jules' Undersea Lodge

Anyway, the whole thing is quite safe, and the suite has 24-hour monitoring by staff and redundant backup systems. Just for making the dive down, you'll have to receive a training course if you aren't a certified diver.

Luxury packages include a "mer-chef" who will scuba down to whip up a nice dinner for you. Couples can even get married after diving into the briny deep. It brings the concept of "taking the plunge" to a whole new level.

There are also medical restrictions on the website to make sure you are healthy enough to make the dive safely. Obviously, as this isn't your average hotel, you must be able to swim as a prerequisite for the visit.

Incidentally, the Jules' Undersea Lodge is named for Jules Verne of *20,000 Leagues Under the Sea* fame.

Celebrities from Canadian Prime Minister Pierre Trudeau to Aerosmith's Steven Tyler have been guests at this establishment.

33

FREE PARKING IN NEW JERSEY

Where can I find the Monopoly game properties in real life?

We all remember the avenues in our hometown, but there is one set of street names almost every kid recalls. Welcome to a part of Secret America where houses are green, hotels are red, and you can buy an entire railroad for just $200.

Monopoly was a mainstay of family game nights from coast to coast, yet many never realized the streets represented on the board are quite real and most still exist—in Atlantic City, New Jersey.

Of course, there have been changes. The Parker Brothers classic was a Depression-era creation, and the ensuing decades have scrambled property values a bit. The light-blue titles were the second cheapest on the board but, according to an AOL.com article from 2010, their fortunes have improved with the Vermont, Oriental, and Connecticut set being "among the city's most valuable areas."

AOL says Park Place and Boardwalk remain, as well, and so do the expensive hotel rooms that ended so many games.

Still, other properties have fallen on hard times. A 2015 Associated Press article noted that parts of Pacific Avenue "are pocked with run-down buildings and streetwalkers,"

In 1972, there was an effort to change the names of the real Baltic and Mediterranean Avenues, but it failed due to public outcry.

In the real world, houses aren't green and hotels aren't red, but this was still most Americans' first experience with real estate investment. Credit: Mark Strozier via Flickr under Creative Commons 2.0

THE MONOPOLY STREETS

WHAT Streets we all know by heart

WHERE Atlantic City, NJ

COST With or without hotels?

PRO TIP Despite the way many players play, the official rules of Monopoly for most of its existence didn't provide a financial windfall if you land on Free Parking. The place was simply a free spot where nothing happens.

leaving it an unlikely candidate for the swanky quarter of the board.

More prosperous is the yellow property set, which AOL reported had a median home value well into the six-figure range. Notably, Marvin Gardens was actually a misspelled version of Marven Gardens, a pricey neighborhood just off Ventnor Avenue. In one of the odder mea culpas ever issued, Parker Brothers finally apologized to Marven Gardens residents in 1995 for the ancient typo.

A few roads are missing altogether. St. Charles Place is gone thanks to casino construction. Illinois Avenue still exists but has since been renamed for civil rights icon Martin Luther King Jr.

After its initial creation as "The Landlord's Game" by a woman named Elizabeth Magie, numerous localized versions with a given area's street names popped up. Charles Darrow, the fellow who popularized it as "Monopoly," just happened to have an Atlantic City set, so that's the one we know today.

34

BIKING THE APOCALYPSE

Where can you see an abandoned turnpike?

In its day, the Pennsylvania Turnpike was something to behold. Opened in 1940, it effectively premiered the idea of a limited-access highway more than a decade before a drop of concrete was poured for the nation's first interstates. The idea was so new that contemporary media reports had to tell people about strange, unfamiliar concepts like interchanges and overpasses. No one knew what these things were yet.

But the 1950s saw the creation of the national interstate system, and as it expanded, it began to incorporate the once-unique turnpike. However, this was not possible where old narrow tunnels had simply become outdated. By 1968, a thirteen-mile central-Pennsylvania portion of the historic highway was bypassed and left to nature.

As the 21st Century dawned, some of this disused pavement was sold for a symbolic $1 to a nonprofit with the aim of eventually turning it into a trail system. Though little was done to reach this goal of creating a biking locale, people began using it as one anyway. It became so popular that The Washington Post even referred to it as "the Pennsylvania Turnbike."

Officially speaking, it is not open to the public. Unofficially speaking, people are free to bike or walk the trail at their

---

Nearby Breezewood, Pennsylvania, is notable for having one of the only discontinuous segments of interstate in the nation. Drivers from I-70 are diverted briefly through town on U.S. Route 30 before rejoining the limited-access highway.

The 1.3-mile Sideling Hill Tunnel exemplifies Pike 2 Bike's motto, "Bike into the Light." Even under the brightest conditions, you can't see the other end when you enter, and it is said to be completely dark inside during fog.
Credit: Murray Schrotenboer

PIKE 2 BIKE ABANDONED TURNPIKE TRAIL

WHAT A post-apocalyptic bike ride

WHERE Access is at the junction of Tannery Rd. and U.S. 30 just east of Breezewood, PA

COST Free on your own. Tour rates vary

PRO TIP Don't enter the tunnels between October and April. You might disturb hibernating bat populations which would be an unpleasant experience for both you and them.

own risk. For a fee, tours are even offered of the former highway by Pike 2 Bike. Described by the group as "the most unique (and strange) ride you will ever do," the affairs run anywhere from three to seven hours and allow participants to see the first road reflectors and rumble strips used in America.

Many decide to do the journey, including two tunnels that can still be accessed, by themselves. But beware, these are longer than they seem, and daylight doesn't filter into the middle. Uneven pavement and other hazards might be encountered inside, and flashlights are considered a must.

"Get a glimpse of America after the apocalypse!" brags the website.

In fact, that's the usual description most people use for the experience, and even Hollywood has taken notice. The lonely highway was used for scenes from the post-apocalypse film *The Road* in 2009.

35

THE IMMORTAL WOMAN

Why is a Virginia tobacco farmer among the most important human beings to ever exist and you've never heard of her?

In Vancouver, Washington, there exists an educational institution called the Henrietta Lacks Health and Bioscience High School. It is not uncommon for schools to be named after famous scientists or doctors—people who've developed treatments for diseases, furthered human knowledge, or advanced the frontier of research. Henrietta Lacks certainly did all of that.

But Lacks was no scientist, nor was she a physician or researcher. In fact, she was a tobacco farmer with no background in science at all. Yet she also happens to be one of the most important humans in the history of medicine.

The scientific part of the story begins in 1951 when Lacks, a young mother, perished of cervical cancer. Samples of her tumor were taken by doctors and processed, but the cells showed a remarkable quality. The culture didn't die. Lacks's cells

HENRIETTA LACKS HEALTH AND BIOSCIENCE HIGH SCHOOL

WHAT An immortal legacy

WHERE 9105 NE 9th St., Vancouver, WA

COST None

NOTEWORTHY Lacks's real name didn't even become public until the 1970s. HeLa was associated with research pseudonyms like Helen Lane or Helen Larsen.

Henrietta Lacks's cells were even sent into space as part of an experiment on the effects of zero-gravity environments.

This school's name is a testament to the importance of Henrietta Lacks' contribution to science. Credit: Courtesy Evergreen Public Schools

are the first—and to this day only—"immortal" human cell line. As such, they became incredibly valuable for research and began to be shared widely. Known as "HeLa" cells, they've become a staple of labs all over the planet, helping to develop drugs for illnesses from hemophilia to herpes, Parkinson's to polio. Whether in cloning or chemotherapy, HeLa cells have been standard equipment on the front lines of medicine for decades.

Rebecca Skloot, author of *The Immortal Life of Henrietta Lacks*, said there is no way to know how many HeLa cells exist, but one researcher estimated that—put together— they would total 50 million metric tons, while another said they could encircle the entire Earth three times.

Regrettably, Lacks's contribution to science was not initially repaid with respect from the scientific community. Her family didn't even know samples had been taken from her until a quarter-century after her death, and the case opened a serious debate over medical ethics.

"HeLa cells were the first human biological materials ever bought and sold, which helped launch a multi-billion dollar industry," Skloot said.

Still, Skloot said the family takes enormous pride in all the lifesaving work that Lacks's cells have made possible.

"They want HeLa cells to continue to do good," she told CNN in 2013. "They just want to be part of the conversation."

36

ICON OF INVENTION

What World War II Hollywood sex symbol is responsible for GPS?

She was legendary for her looks in the 1930s and 1940s, with her seductive eyes lighting up such films as *Algiers* and *Samson and Delilah*, but Hollywood actress Hedy Lamarr was far more than skin deep. Her all-too-often untold story is an unusual one that tells of sexism, torpedoes, and player pianos, and results in the communications technology you now rely on every day.

If you like Wi-Fi, Bluetooth or GPS, thank Hedy Lamarr.

Born in Austria, Lamarr left Europe for more promising shores in America and quickly became a hit. But the famous actress never lost the urge for her true passion—inventing. Along with George Antheil, a composer who had a talent for more than music, she created the idea for "frequency-hopping," which aimed to defeat attempts to jam radio signals. The pair believed the invention, which was inspired by an effort to make player pianos work in unison, might be used to help guide torpedoes to their targets at sea, a particularly pressing issue in 1942.

However, the U.S. Navy wasn't impressed with the concept and preferred her war bond fundraising sex appeal to her engineering abilities. It got little attention at the

***

Many still recall the name of this famous actress from Harvey Korman's character "Hedley Lamarr" in Mel Brooks' comedic "Blazing Saddles". Lamarr found the joke less than funny. She sued for invasion of privacy.

Hedy Lamarr wasn't just another pretty face. She helped shape the modern communications revolution. Credit: Reznor Hawkthrone via Flickr under public domain

NATIONAL INVENTORS HALL OF FAME MUSEUM

WHAT Beauty and brains

WHERE 600 Dulany St., Alexandria, VA

COST Free

NOTEWORTHY Lamarr's original first name was "Hedwig."

time. However, the idea would eventually be adopted by the military during the Cuban Missile Crisis and was later reborn as wireless technology began to take off in the late 20th century. Lamarr and Antheil's "spread-spectrum" signals laid the foundation for your smartphone.

As for Lamarr, her career dimmed as she aged. By the late 1950s she was out of films entirely, and a failed plastic surgery attempt left her reclusive.

Her contributions to technology weren't even discovered until the 1990s, just a few years before her death. According to an NPR account, she accepted an award related to her invention by saying simply, "Well, it's about time."

Today, in addition to being on Hollywood's Walk of Fame, Lamarr is in the National Inventors Hall of Fame, having been posthumously inducted with her co-creator Anthiel in 2014. You can visit the institution's museum in Alexandria, Virginia.

37

ALL QUIET ON THE WEST VIRGINIA FRONT

What is the National Radio Quiet Zone?

As you read these words, the Earth is bathed in electromagnetic waves. Some emanate from alien galaxies and spend millions of years traversing the vast void of space to bring us faint signals, cryptic clues to the nature of the universe and the mysteries of stars too far to see or imagine.

And it'd be a shame if they got wiped out by someone's Wi-Fi downloading funny cat videos.

That's why we have the National Radio Quiet Zone, a surprisingly massive 13,000-square-mile rectangle covering a chunk of the Virginia/West Virginia border. Inside the zone, radio emissions are strictly controlled to hold down local interference for the sake of the Green Bank Observatory. In areas within a ten-mile radius of the huge telescope, Wi-Fi is mostly banned, and smartphones go out of service. The closer you get to the observatory, the tighter the restrictions become. As *National Geographic* noted in 2014, employees at the telescope can't even microwave their own lunch. A *Wired* article said that older, diesel-powered vehicles free of electronics are used at the facility itself, since even spark plugs can cause interference.

"The types of energies we look at are less than the energy of a single snowflake falling on the earth," one Green Bank astronomer told NPR in 2013.

Nearby Sugar Grove, West Virginia, hosts receiving radio facilities for the United States Navy, which also takes advantage of the zone.

This spot in West Virginia is one of the last places in modern America where smartphones don't rule the day. Credit: Michael J. Holstine/Green Bank Observatory

THE GREEN BANK OBSERVATORY

WHAT The sound of silence

WHERE 155 Observatory Rd., Green Bank, WV

COST Tours of the Green Bank facility are $6 for adults

PRO TIP Check greenbankobservatory.org/events to look for special tours that showcase parts of the telescope not normally open to the public.

The laws have been in place since 1958, and while one local ski lodge has reportedly found a way to offer cell service and even Wi-Fi using very low-power transmission equipment, statutes have generally kept this area as electromagnetism-free as anything in the modern world can get. This is among the few places pay phones still exist, since land lines are the primary mode of communication. The near-universal sight of folks gaping at mobile devices is absent here.

Aside from a certain quaintness it lends to the tiny Wi-Fi-less town of Green Bank, the Quiet Zone has been a godsend for individuals who suffer from sensitivity to electromagnetism. Although the malady hasn't been confirmed as an illness by medical science, sufferers say that the modern world's cacophony of RF signals is a living nightmare for them, causing everything from stomach discomfort to intense headaches. Some have moved to the zone in order to get a respite from the world of invisible waves that the rest of us seem so unable to live without.

38 THE GREAT MOLASSES FLOOD

Were several blocks of Boston once destroyed by a deadly tidal wave of molasses?

At first telling, it sounds like a hoax, something that just could not possibly be true—an urban legend, perhaps, a bit of parody or maybe just a joke of epic proportions.

But the unassuming plaque along a Commercial Street stone wall proves otherwise, and on January 15, 1919, it was certainly no laughing matter. That was the day when several blocks of Massachusetts's largest city were devastated by a flood tide of molasses that left twenty-one people dead in the wake of one of the most bizarre industrial disasters in the planet's history.

The strange catastrophe occurred around lunchtime at the Purity Distilling Company when a 50-foot-tall holding tank failed, instantly dispensing over two million gallons of molasses into the unsuspecting streets of Boston. Witnesses reported a 15- to 50-foot wave of the sticky brown goo. For all the similes about the slowness

THE BOSTON MOLASSES FLOOD PLAQUE

WHAT A tsunami of molasses

WHERE Commercial St. east of Charter St., Boston, MA

COST None

NOTEWORTHY About 3,000 witnesses testified in the resulting court cases, which took roughly six years to hear.

The United States Industrial Alcohol Company eventually paid about $7,000 to the family of each of the victims.

The Boston Daily Globe *covers one of America's most bizarre industrial disasters.* Credit: Boston Public Library via Flickr under Creative Commons 2.0

of molasses in January, the speed of the substance was remarkable. According to an account from *Mental Floss*, it traveled at thirty-five miles per hour, a rate "sufficient to rip buildings off of their foundations." Homes were crushed, wagons were washed away, horses were drowned, and an elevated train track was destroyed as the tsunami flattened a two-block area. One estimate put damage in the $100 million range in today's money.

A staggering 80,000 man-hours were required for cleanup of the disaster, which spawned over one hundred lawsuits against the company over the molasses tank's defective and incompetent construction. In an indication of how negligent the owners had been, their apparent solution to ongoing leakage from the molasses vat was to paint it brown to cut down on the visibility of the problem.

Even beyond the disaster zone, Boston was inundated with people walking out of the area tracking molasses behind them as they went. Whether it was the power of suggestion or not, some claimed the area still smelled sweet as late as the 1980s.

39

A DIVIDED BANNER

Why does Maryland's state flag contain a symbol that was once illegal to display in the state?

State flags are a seemingly endless source of trivia, pride, and derision. Utah's is centered on a beehive. Oregon's has a beaver on the back, and Missouri's appears to be inexplicably obsessed with bears. Virginia may have the nation's most aggressive flag. Featuring a sword-bearing figure standing with foot planted proudly upon the chest of a slain ruler, the Roman-inspired emblem is the only one in the country to effectively feature a homicide in progress.

But perhaps no state flag has quite the élan of Maryland's. Divided into quarters, the banner alternates a vivid yellow-and-black checker pattern with a red-and-white cross bottony. No doubt more than one wag has noted its resemblance to the offspring of a heraldic emblem and a stock car racing flag. But love it or hate it, its eye-catching patterns and sharply contrasting colors certainly set it apart from virtually any other state banner.

Another unique feature is that part of this flag could have once gotten you arrested in Maryland just for flying it.

The issue goes back to the Civil War, when Maryland was one of the biggest headaches on Abraham Lincoln's mind. It was bad enough that the federal capital was perched on the lip of rebellious Virginia, but it was also sandwiched to the north by slaveholding Maryland, which was rife with Confederate sentiment. Situated just one hundred

---

Some of the gravestones of Confederate soldiers from Maryland still bear the cross bottony as a symbol of the cause for which they perished.

MARYLAND STATE CAPITOL

WHAT A symbol of old divisions and new unity

WHERE 100 State Cir., Annapolis, MD

COST None

NOTEWORTHY Completed in 1779, Maryland's State House is the oldest such building still being used by a legislature.

miles from the rebel capital, Washington, D.C., must have sometimes felt like an island of Unionism in a sea of Southern sentiment.

The history of the flag dates to the state's Colonial days, when the two symbols represented different branches of the family of George Calvert, founder of Baltimore. But during the war, those insignia began to identify sectionalist sympathies. Unionist Marylanders took to the yellow-and-black, while their fraternal opponents began wearing the cross. Freedom of speech was rather brutally suppressed during the war, and being a Southern sympathizer was not considered a protected political opinion. By one account, more civilian arrests took place in Maryland than in any other state. The bottony became effectively illegal to show, and displaying it could land you in jail.

Of course, after the war, sentiment softened and grudges needed to heal. In Maryland, that meant mending wounds by reuniting the disparate symbols that had divided the state, which endorsed the new flag in 1904. Whatever its starkly clashing color scheme may imply about the past, today it represents "unity in the community," as one state archivist told *The Baltimore Sun* in 1997.

40

CHOPPED CHICKEN

Why does a Colorado town celebrate a headless chicken each year?

Borne of many a farmland experience with poultry preparation, the phrase "like a chicken with its head cut off" has become a standard cliché over the years. But few of those fowl ever had much recognition marking their sacrifice beyond a few compliments to the chef after the following day's dinner.

However, that was not to be the case for one beheaded bird who managed to keep his cool despite losing his head.

The story of the bird who would become known as Mike the Headless Chicken began where most stories about barnyard chickens end. Mike's September 1945 decapitation at the hands of his owner, Lloyd Olsen, should have ended his life, but shockingly, the animal did not die. Apparently, Mike was made of sterner stuff, and the mere loss of his cranium did little to slow him down.

As it would turn out, the survival of "Miracle Mike" was actually the result of Olsen's mother-in-law, who evidently had a taste for chicken necks such that Olsen attempted to make the cut as high as possible. The chop left Mike with a bit of a brain stem, despite losing his higher functions.

Mike's durability may seem a singular example, but actually, less complex creatures simply don't require as much brain to survive. Despite being unable to take in food or water, beheaded cockroaches can survive perfectly well

---

Chicken consumption in the United States has been rising since the 1950s, and in 2014 it overtook beef as the nation's most popular meat.

Where else but Fruita, Colorado, could you see a giant decapitated chicken riding a hoverboard?
Credit: Courtesy Fruita Parks and Recreation

MIKE THE HEADLESS CHICKEN FESTIVAL

WHAT Proof that brains are overrated

WHERE Fruita, CO

COST The concerts are free to attend

PRO TIP When in Fruita, be sure to check out the rugged Western landscapes of the nearby Colorado National Monument.

for days based on the function of their nervous system. Losing a head doesn't impede a roach's busy social life.

Mike's social life actually improved. For a year and a half, the fowl became a mid-century version of a viral sensation, going on national tours where Olsen described him as a fine chicken "except for not having a head."

Unfortunately, Mike's time in the spotlight was limited. While on tour, the prize bird accidentally choked to death while being fed with an eyedropper.

But Mike's indomitable determination to live through one of history's most efficient forms of execution is now immortalized by the good people of Fruita, Colorado, who hold an annual festival in his honor. The event, which includes live music, a 5k run, and a disc golf tournament, was set to celebrate its 19th year in 2017.

41 BUTTER BATTLES

Why was margarine required to be pink in some states?

Butter or margarine? For some, the choice is sacred. For others, it is just whatever they grab off the shelf first.

But butter was big business for millions of American farmers and, for many years, margarine was something akin to a mortal enemy. The legislative and public relations wars fought between the two were less pleasant than eating a tub of unflavored yogurt.

According to *National Geographic*, a Minnesota governor termed margarine products as "abominations" wrought by "depraved human genius," and Sen. Joseph Quarles of neighboring Wisconsin said he refused to accept butter substitutes "matured under the chill of death."

Quarles's stomping ground was pretty much ground zero in the butter battles. Famous for all things dairy, the Badger State was one of those to initially ban oleo outright when the European innovation hit U.S. shores. After that became untenable, it passed a welter of laws designed to tax or restrict margarine. When all else failed, butter-boosting legislators tried to make oleo substitutes unappealing by prohibiting yellow coloration in margarine. *National Geographic* says some went a step further and MANDATED

In 2017, the Associated Press reported on a suit filed against Wisconsin's butter grading system by angry consumers alleging that they were unable to get their favorite brand of Irish butter without crossing state lines to acquire it.

The Upper Midwest isn't known for its fiery tempers, but when it came to what Americans smear on their toast each morning, dairy farmers had very strong opinions. Credit: Pixabay

BUTTER LAWS

WHAT The war over oleo

WHERE Wisconsin and the Upper Midwest

COST Check your local supermarket

NOTEWORTHY Margarine was invented by Frenchman Hippolyte Mége-Mouriés in 1869 as a cheaper substitute for butter. He sold the patent and died broke.

oleo coloration in such unappetizing colors as pink or black. The situation became so ludicrous that some margarine makers took to the practice of including dye packs so you could color your own spread. Meanwhile, high taxes caused margarine smuggling operations among housewives.

Over time, public acceptance grew, federal protectionist measures faded, and even Wisconsin began to see the light. It was the last to drop its anti-yellow law in 1967.

Still, as of fairly recently, some anti-margarine measures were still on the books. Despite a 2011 attempt to amend it, the state still had a law that said restaurants could not offer margarine instead of butter unless requested. Yet, the *Fond du Lac Reporter* noted in 2015 that the Restaurant Association interpreted the law to simply mean that butter must be available if margarine is.

And butter fans say there may be other benefits of a Wisconsin law mandating butter in the state's correctional facilities. Perhaps the prisoners like it.

"That's one benefit of serving time in Wisconsin," one butter producer told the *Milwaukee Journal-Sentinel*.

HOG WILD (page 118)

A LITTLE GREEN (page 130)

CAR-FREE IS CAREFREE (page 6)

"NOBODY SHOT ME" (page 140)

FROZEN DEAD GUY DAYS (page 150)

MEETING AT THE TRIPOINT (page 170)

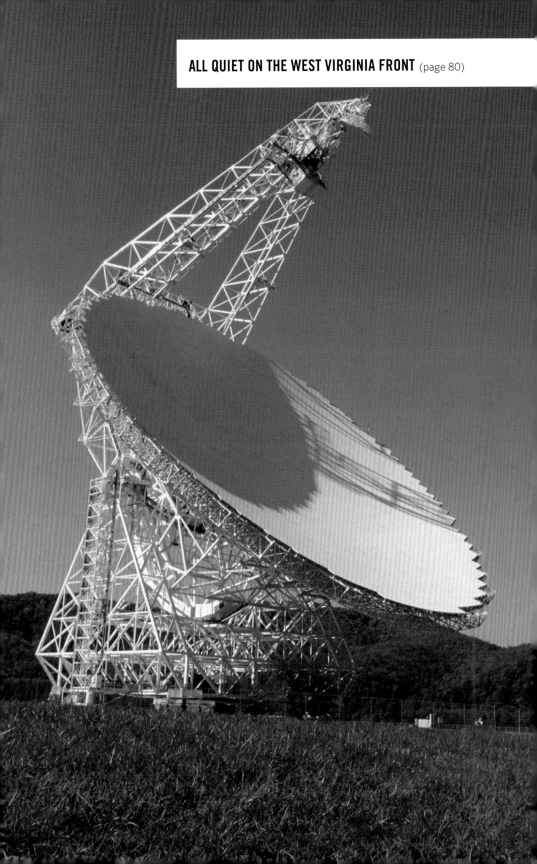

ALL QUIET ON THE WEST VIRGINIA FRONT (page 80)

BIKING THE APOCALYPSE (page 74)

NO HOLIER PLACE (page 154)

"PLANTED UP TO THE VERY DOOR" (page 22)

LIFE ON THE LINE (page 176)

MAN OF THE PEOPLE (page 148)

42 HIGHWAY TO THE DANGER ZONE

Does a small area exist in Idaho where laws don't apply due to a constitutional loophole?

The United States is a nation of laws, and not all of them are about butter. But as any good lawyer knows, that also means we are a nation of loopholes. According to one law professor, one of those loopholes could theoretically leave someone able to commit a crime without fear of punishment as long as that person does so along a small stretch of land in Idaho hugging the state's border with Wyoming.

The problem pertains to Yellowstone National Park. Most think of Yellowstone as an entirely Wyoming-based affair, and the vast majority of the park is indeed within the boundaries of that state. But the north edge of America's first declared national park doesn't actually end at the border. It overlaps into Montana, while a couple of miles of the western edge fall just within the bounds of Idaho.

So, what's the problem?

Well, back in 2005, law professor Brian Kalt noted that the Sixth Amendment to the Constitution guarantees the

---

Kalt said that before 1548, some individuals did get away with murder in England by committing the crime in one county but making sure the victim died in a different one.

Is a narrow strip of Yellowstone National Park actually an anarchic zone of lawlessness where all manner of mayhem is legal? Probably not, but that's why most of us didn't go to law school.
Credit: Pixabay

right to a trial by jury "of the State and district wherein the crime shall have been committed." The district for Yellowstone, set long ago, is the federal court for Wyoming. But since the fringes of said park overlap into other states, it creates an accidental conundrum. The area of Idaho within the park is only two miles in width but—at least in theory—any jury pool for a crime committed there could not be drawn from anywhere else in Idaho because that wouldn't be in the same district, and it couldn't be drawn from anywhere else in the Wyoming district because the rest of it isn't in the same state. Only jurors from the narrow strip would be eligible to serve.

But no one actually lives there—at least according to the professor's claims in 2005, when he made a bit of a splash in the media by publishing an article on the situation. The issue probably came about because the park established its borders in 1872, which is considerably before any of the states involved did.

So what's the real story?

Dubbed rather melodramatically as the "zone of death" by the BBC and the "Yellowstone Murder Zone" by FOX News, the truth is that the perfect crime probably doesn't await anyone in Idaho, as Kalt outlines in a section entitled "Don't Go Killing Anyone Just Yet." Someone planning or preparing for a crime in the so-called "zone" could be guilty of making said preparations in another jurisdiction. Moreover, Kalt admits that courts might easily dismiss such a mechanistic interpretation of the law anyway. So don't commit any crimes thinking you'll get off free as a bird. As both media outlets noted, it probably isn't a lawless bastion of anarchy.

However, the professor averred that he still won't be planning a visit anytime soon.

"I'm not going there for a million dollars," he told one news station.

Yellowstone National Park may be halfway between the equator and the North Pole, but—according to one legal scholar—part of it exists in a lawless netherworld. Credit: David Baugher

43 ONLINE ORIGINS

What was the first message ever sent on the internet, and can you see the room where it happened?

The numbers are startling: According to Internetlivestats.com, more than . . .

2.5 million emails, 68,000 YouTube views, 59,000 Google searches, 7,500 tweets, 2,500 Skype calls, 1,200 Tumblr posts and 700 Instagram photos all traversed the internet . . .

. . . in a single second . . . every second . . . as of March 2017.

THE ROOM WHERE THE INTERNET WAS BORN

WHAT The place that allows you to spend three hours a day binge-watching Netflix

WHERE 3420 Boelter Hall, UCLA Campus, Los Angeles, Calif.

COST None

NOTEWORTHY There are more active users on Pinterest as of March 2017 then there were people in the entire Roman Empire at its height.

The internet is a big place but—like all big things—it started small. Whether the Information Superhighway has an end, no one can say, but it certainly has a beginning, and it all started right here. The internet was born in Room 3420 of Boelter Hall on the UCLA campus at 10:30 p.m. on October 29, 1969, where a small cadre of researchers sent the first message into the digital ether.

What did they send? A passage from Hemingway? Part of the Gettysburg Address? A verse from Genesis? Nope.

They sent "LO." It was supposed to be "LOGIN," but the computer crashed. So much for a "Watson, come here" kind of moment. Still, those two characters kicked off a revolution that made

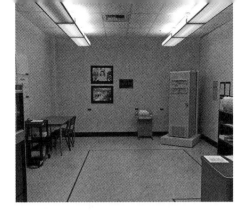

The pastel paint and institutional décor may not seem exciting but if it weren't for this room, you'd never get your daily supply of cat videos, email scams and angry Facebook political arguments between people you didn't even like back when you had to put up with them in high school. Credit: Amy Akmal/UCLA Henry Samueli School of Engineering and Applied Science

Gutenberg's printing press look like a minor advancement in copying technology.

Anyway, after rebooting things, they sent the internet's second message, a spam ad for penis enlargement pills.

Just kidding.

You can visit Room 3420, and the campus has even restored it to its pristine 1969 condition. That includes the actual original Interface Message Processor—which looks about the size of a doublewide high school locker—that sent that first message to the Stanford Research Institute.

Today, the center that manages the room is named for computer scientist Leonard Kleinrock, who was instrumental in the development of "packet switching" technology, which would soon become the backbone of the new communications network.

Odd as it might seem, no one even comprehended the ramifications of the message that started it all. Creating ARPANET, the forerunner for today's internet might have seemed a neat project, but there was no way to predict the explosion of information it would create.

"We didn't even take a picture," Kleinrock told *Gizmodo* in 2014.

There were four "nodes" in the initial ARPANET, of which UCLA was one. By 1981, there were more than 200.

44 THE WEST WINGS

Why don't bald eagles sound anything like you think they do?

It is a scene any American can conjure in his or her mind—a wide prairie of windblown wheat ripples against an awe-inspiring backdrop of purple mountains majesty, while above the terrain soars the noblest of avians, a bald eagle that sends a powerful, chilling screech echoing across the landscape.

It's a beautiful image.

But the noise you just played in your head is a lie. Despite what you've seen and heard on TV, the bald eagle's piercing call is a myth. Eagles don't actually sound like that. Though they might look regal enough and they are indeed very effective predators, the voice of our national symbol is something closer to a squeaky squeal on the high end of the pitch range.

So what have you been listening to?

"They dub over it with a red-tailed hawk's cry," one bird expert told NPR in 2012.

Well, after all, who wants a high-pitched warble to echo across the landscape, and who would cheer for a local high school team nicknamed "The Squeakin' Eagles"? Genuine ornithology can really be a buzzkill when it comes to patriotic fervor.

But, at least we know our founders loved the bald eagle. Okay, not ALL of our founders did.

"For my own part, I wish the Bald Eagle had not been chosen the Representative of our Country," Ben Franklin

Hawaii is the only U.S. state where bald eagles do not reside.

Sure, he looks noble and majestic but Ben Franklin hated him. Credit: Pixabay

CHILKAT BALD EAGLE PRESERVE

WHAT Birds of a feather

WHERE Alaska Chilkat Bald Eagle Preserve outside Haines, AK

COST Patriotic illusions

PRO TIP Visit between October and February for the largest concentration of eagles.

once wrote. "He is a Bird of bad moral Character. He does not get his living honestly."

The curmudgeonly inventor accused our beloved national symbol of stealing prey from more industrious predators, terming him "poor," "lousy," and "a rank coward" that could be frightened off by a determined sparrow.

According to a 2013 piece by *Smithsonian* magazine, it is a myth that Franklin suggested a turkey replace the eagle, although he did note that the gobbler was "a more respectable bird" that wouldn't hesitate to attack the British should they invade his farmyard.

Franklin was a man of strong opinions.

Anyway, if your reverence for this avian hasn't been completely dimmed by this nugget of Secret America, you will be happy to know that there are lots of places for you to go visit him. The eagle capital of the United States is probably the Alaska Chilkat Bald Eagle Preserve near Haines, Alaska. Created in 1982, it covers 48,000 acres and bills itself as hosting the world's largest concentration of bald eagles.

SMALL-TOWN LIFE

Where is America's smallest incorporated town?

There are a lot of small towns in Secret America, but it is fair to say that none of them are smaller than Monowi, Nebraska. This Boyd County village is situated along State Route 12 just a few miles south of the Missouri River, which marks the South Dakota border. Like people, towns are said to have a personality. If so, this one takes only a single person to define. That's because Elsie Eiler isn't just mayor and primary business owner of this little hamlet—she also happens to be its only resident.

That status has its advantages. Owner of the local tavern, Eiler is empowered to renew her own liquor license in her role as city clerk.

"Essentially, she holds hearings for herself and in theory could voice opposition to herself, if she wanted," said a CBS story on Monowi in 2006. "Only people from the town are allowed to attend the hearing."

But Eiler isn't lonely. Plenty of customers from the surrounding areas like to stop by for a drink or a bit of conversation at her establishment. The food and beverages are supposed to be top notch, and all thirty-five Google reviews were five stars.

In 2013, the unincorporated town of Buford, Wyoming—boasting a population of one—was purchased by a Vietnamese businessman who wished to start selling PhinDeli-brand coffee. He renamed Buford "PhinDeli Town Buford."

The population of Monowi has fallen since this photo was taken. It is down to one. Credit: Brian Kell via Wikimedia

The bar isn't the only institution in town either. Eiler also runs a local library with 5,000 books that honors the vision of her late husband, Rudy, who was quite a bibliophile. The library has a sign that says "Rudy's Dream Come True."

Monowi originally appeared on maps just after the turn of the last century, thanks to the railroad. Its heyday was in 1930, when census figures showed a whopping 123 people inhabiting its borders, but population began to fall off. The post office closed in 1971, and six years later the rail line shut down. By 1980, only eighteen people called Monowi home. Eiler has been the sole resident since 2004.

Today, it does indeed have a sign at the border: "Monowi," it says, with the numeral "1" below it. Moreover, the little town still generates attention from time to time. A 2010 effort by Larry Whitney of "Larry, the Cable Guy" fame brought a thousand folks to town and helped make repairs to local infrastructure.

And so the town continues.

"I'm not going anywhere," Eiler told CBS.

46 HOG WILD

How did a dispute over a dead pig bring Britain to the brink of war with the United States?

The National Park Service website introduces San Juan Island National Historical Park as a place that "celebrates how individuals and nations can resolve disputes without resorting to violence." Perhaps so, but the odd story behind this Washington State site may just as easily make one wonder at how quickly very silly disputes between individuals and nations can escalate to the point where violence becomes a possibility.

Such is the case with the so-called "Pig War," in which a deceased swine almost brought about combat between two nations.

The issue began with ambiguities in the 1846 Treaty of Oregon, which was supposed to set a border between British Canada and the growing American presence in the Pacific Northwest. One area at stake was fifty-five-square-mile San Juan Island, where both nations had set up camp. In June 1859 a British-owned pig was caught digging in the garden of Lyman Cutlar, who unceremoniously shot the animal. The British threatened to arrest the American, and the local U.S. commander sent soldiers in, causing the British to respond by steaming three warships into the area.

The buildup dragged on, attracting the attention of British Admiral Lambert Baynes, who was horrified to find that war might occur "over a squabble about a pig."

Left: The British flag still flies proudly over the old English camp on San Juan Island but this remains American territory despite the sacrifice of some Canadian bacon. Credit: Courtesy of San Juan Island National Historical Park

Washington, D.C., was no happier, since by the end of August, more than 450 Americans were dug in with twenty-two cannons against a British force with fifty-two guns. President James Buchanan sent General Winfield Scott to the area to determine what was going on and figure out how to stop it before it got any worse. By November, tempers had cooled and the Americans ultimately won the island's arbitration, leaving a strange historical footnote and a martyred British pig that sadly died in vain.

The initial American forces sent to the area during the Pig War were under the command of a young captain, George Pickett, who would later become famous in the ill-fated Pickett's Charge, which effectively sealed the Confederate defeat at the Battle of Gettysburg.

OF PARAMOUNT IMPORTANCE

Which mountain inspired one of the most famous movie company logos of all time?

With its fine ski country and unique rock formations, the State of Utah is quite well known for its rugged terrain. Its national parks, slopes, and scenic areas attracted more than 23 million people in 2012, and a survey of the ten most popular tourist spots in the state found that nine of them were natural areas.

But ironically, one formation of natural beauty not found in the top ten is probably the one you've seen whether you've been to the Beehive State or not. That's because Ben Lomond, a 9,700-foot-tall peak in the Wasatch Mountain Range has been appearing in theaters coast to coast for decades—or at least a representation inspired by it has. This high point outside Ogden is allegedly the source for the star-encircled mountain in the Paramount logo. The mountain apparently owes its fame to William Hodkinson, an Ogden-area movie heavyweight who sketched the peak on a napkin in 1914, the same year that Paramount was created out of its predecessor, Famous Players Film Company. Ben Lomond may not be the only mountain he drew on for inspiration, however. Some sources claim that the Paramount logo came from Pike's Peak in Colorado.

Ben Lomond is not "Mt. Ben Lomond" or "Ben Lomond Peak" because "Ben" actually refers to the word "mount" or "mountain" in Scottish.

It isn't surrounded by stars but, viewed from a certain angle, Ben Lomond does indeed look a bit like the Paramount peak. Credit: Brenton Cooper via Flickr under Creative Commons 2.0

BEN LOMOND

WHAT A mountain on the silver screen

WHERE Visible from Ogden, UT

COST None.

PRO TIP The trail to the mountain leaves from near North Fork Park in the Liberty, Utah, area.

In 2008, the *Deseret News* quoted the studio as saying that the insignia was even older than "Leo," the slightly more famous lion that has roared at the beginning of MGM films since around 1916.

Incidentally, the stars surrounding the mountain were supposed to represent the number of stars the studio had under contract at its founding, although that number seems to vary between twenty-two and twenty-four, depending on the source, and various Paramount logos have had different numbers.

Anyway, *Time* magazine reported in 2012 that the old mountain was swapped out for a Peruvian peak in the most recent variations of the insignia.

48 THE NATION'S BUSIEST EMPTY PLACE

Why does one of the most valuable office buildings on the planet house almost no offices?

It is said that fame can leave one empty inside, and for at least one structure in the heart of New York City, that couldn't be truer. The narrow, wedge-shaped Times Square Tower, hidden behind its trademark collection of flashing billboards, is among the most well-known images of New York City, particularly on New Year's Eve, when multitudes gather outside along Seventh and Broadway to watch a glorified disco ball wend its way down to welcome in the new calendar.

But if the vividly lit advertising entombing this famous twenty-five-story edifice embodies the liveliness of the Big Apple, then it also hides a strangely dormant interior.

Almost no one occupies the inside of One Times Square.

According to a 2014 *Business Insider* article, the building has a couple of tenants and some storage space, but it is pretty desolate beyond that. A *New Yorker* tour of the spot found "abandoned floors" that were "littered with graffiti and the remnants of old signs."

It wasn't always this way. Built just after the turn of the century, this very iconic part of Secret America was once home to *The New York Times* and housed other entities over the years.

Electric advertising arrived in Times Square in 1917.

122

Even among the welter of bright lights that define the heart of Manhattan, One Times Square (at center) stands out.
Credit: Pixabay

TIMES SQUARE TOWER

WHAT A building of billboards

WHERE One Times Square, New York, NY

COST $1.1 million to $4 million a year for an ad, according to 2012 figures

NOTEWORTHY The idea of dropping a ball originated because a ban on fireworks in 1907 put the kibosh on the usual pyrotechnics that *The New York Times* used to welcome the new year.

But in 1995, new ownership found a better use for the building than housing people. Instead, it would house ads, which was not a bad plan for a spot visible to about 100 million pedestrians annually—along with pretty much everyone else in the country on December 31.

In 2012 it brought in a cool $23 million in revenue just from advertising and had an estimated value that could approach half-a-billion dollars.

With numbers like that, who needs occupants?

49

THE BURNING TOWN

How has a town been on fire for more than fifty years?

Just off Pennsylvania State Route 61, you'll find a strange disused portion of two-lane road spattered and coated with virtually every color a can of spray paint might emit. Known as "The Graffiti Highway," it attracts visitors for its oddness but it also tells a story. It is the sad tale of nearby Centralia, Pennsylvania, once a city of 1,000 people and today a tragic footnote in the history of environmental disasters.

That's because Centralia is on fire—and has been on fire for more than half a century.

The strange story of the town's demise begins with a botched 1962 attempt to burn some garbage. Unfortunately, the blaze invaded an old anthracite mine and the coal inside caught fire. Sometime later, residents started noticing unusual things about their home. One woman noted that she was able to grow produce in December thanks to a "self-heating garden."

But what was happening was the spread of a monstrous fire underground, one that proved impossible to control and eventually began belching toxic fumes, creating steaming sinkholes and buckling roads. The Graffiti Highway is a stretch of the now redirected Route 61.

CENTRALIA'S GRAFFITI HIGHWAY

WHAT A paint-covered highway and a ghost town

WHERE Off State Rte. 61, just south of Centralia, PA

COST None

PRO TIP Be aware that underground coal fires are dangerous. Sudden sinkholes and toxic fumes can present serious hazards. As Centraliapa.org notes, if you visit the town, be respectful. These were once people's homes and property and people still have loved ones buried in local cemeteries. Don't litter, trespass, or add graffiti.

This abandoned section of old Route 61 is now a lonely message board in the Pennsylvania forest, thanks to an underground coal fire that will keep burning for decades. Credit: Kevin Jarrett via Flickr under Creative Commons 2.0

But the highway wasn't the toxic fire's only victim. By the 1980s, virtually the whole town had to be evacuated after various attempts to fight the underground blaze failed. According to Centraliapa.org, only five residents remained as of 2017. The conflagration is expected to burn for another 250 years.

As strange as this story sounds, its most unusual aspect may be that it really isn't unusual at all. According to a May 2005 article in *Smithsonian* magazine, at least thirty-eight such underground coal fires were burning out of control *in Pennsylvania alone*. Hundreds of others dot the country, while energy-hungry nations like China have many more, with some believing that the smoldering blazes could be having a measurable effect on global warming. One geologist calls it "a worldwide catastrophe."

Australia is home to the world's oldest naturally occurring underground coal fire, which has been burning for an estimated 6,000 years.

50

DELI MEATS IN SPACE

How did the first corned beef sandwich in orbit prompt a congressional hearing?

Gravity is one of those things we tend to take for granted, so we don't always think about the complex mechanics of simple things that astronauts have to worry over. From exercise to urination, not everything is easy in a weightless environment. Certainly, enjoying a good meal outside the envelope of Earth's atmosphere qualifies on that score.

And that's how, in the early days of space travel, a smuggled corned beef on rye became the subject of a congressional inquiry.

The story stems from an incident aboard the 1965 flight of Gemini 3, when pilot John Young brought the hitherto uncontroversial sandwich aboard the craft after purchasing it from a shop at a nearby Ramada Inn. He then produced it as a surprise meal for Commander Virgil "Gus" Grissom.

Unfortunately, the sandwich, designed for the high-gravity environment of the Ramada Inn, quickly began to disintegrate in the weightlessness of the space capsule, a fact that could have presented problems if crumbs had gotten into any of the high-tech equipment.

"It was a thought, anyway," said Young.

"Yep," replied Grissom.

"Not a very good one," admitted Young, possibly sensing the potential problems his unauthorized snack might create for the mission.

Congress agreed with him and even held a hearing on the matter once everyone was back on the ground. In part, the legislators were angered at the thought that the astronauts were not eating the specially made foods they were supposed to be testing.

Surprisingly, however, this wasn't the last corned beef in space. The dish did end up on the approved list for a 1981

Virgil I. Grissom may have been the first man to attempt to eat a corned beef sandwich in zero gravity. It did not go well. But you can still visit the sandwich—assuming for some reason you'd want to. Credit: NASA

mission that was ironically helmed by Young. It is unknown if the commander influenced the menu.

As for the sandwich, its fate remains murky. *Smithsonian* magazine says it is displayed in acrylic at the Virgil I. Grissom Memorial in Indiana. However, *Popular Mechanics* believes that that exhibit must be a replica sandwich because the real McCoy was partially eaten. The mystery remains.

Perhaps congressional hearings are in order.

Contrary to popular belief, Tang, the famous fruit-flavored drink, was neither invented by NASA nor designed for use in space. It was simply a preexisting commercial product that the agency began using.

51 THE BAD BOY OF KRYPTON

Was America's greatest superhero originally evil?

It is said that power corrupts and absolute power corrupts absolutely. Thus, we are left with the paradox of Superman. Though presented as relentlessly honorable, it seems that someone as invincible as the Man of Steel would be tempted to turn his awesome abilities to evil ends eventually. After all, he's only human.

Well, Kryptonian, anyway.

So why wouldn't Superman be driven to selfish designs by his powers?

Surprisingly, that was precisely how he was originally conceived. That's right. The foremost crusader for truth, justice, and the American way was actually supposed to be a bad guy.

As aficionados of the genre know, Superman first debuted in a 1938 issue of *Action Comics*. But his original character dates to several years earlier, when teenagers Jerry Siegel and Joe Shuster first sketched out their idea for a Nietzschean-style Übermench who used his incredible powers for his own benefit and owed far more to Lex Luthor than to Clark Kent.

In some respects, this may have struck a bit too close to reality for comfort. As Jewish Virtual Library notes, Superman's creators, both of whom were Jewish, initially published their sci-fi story in 1933, the same year Adolf Hitler assumed power

---

THE HOUSE WHERE SUPERMAN WAS BORN

WHAT Superman's place

WHERE 10622 Kimberly Ave.

COST None

PRO TIP This is a private home. Don't trespass or bother anyone.

Any good superhero needs a dark side, and Superman is no exception. He was initially conceived of as a villainous character rather than a good guy . . . and you can still visit the house in Cleveland where he was created. Credit: Pixabay

in Germany. Hitler's philosophy of racial superiority owed a good deal to a very dark and somewhat butchered version of Nietzsche's ideas, and the Nazis' idealism of an Aryan "superman" was born partly from it.

Whatever the case, Siegel and Shuster's story fared poorly, and their lead character was eventually recast in a less morally unappealing light.

Anyway, while Superman may have been born on Krypton and raised in Smallville, his real roots lie in the Glenville area of Cleveland. The house on Kimberly Avenue where Siegel grew up might not be the Fortress of Solitude, but it actually bears a version of the iconic "S" on its fence, and Kimberly itself has been subtitled Jerry Siegel Lane. Nearby Parkwood Drive has been humorously given the moniker "Lois Lane." There is also an historical marker at St. Clair Avenue and E. 105th Street.

DC Comics paid just $130 for the rights to Superman—part of a $412 check to Siegel and Shuster. The canceled check was sold in 2012 for $160,000. The company misspelled both men's names on the document.

52

A LITTLE GREEN

Where is the planet's smallest park?

The United States is home to thousands of local parks, many of them meandering through suburban areas or sprawling in small towns.

But it is urban areas where people really have to get creative when it comes to recreational green space. Large tracts of parkland aren't always available between big buildings amidst the dense grid of crowded avenues. You have to take what you can get.

Just ask the good folks of Portland, Oregon, home to Mill Ends Park, which, at two feet in diameter, has been recognized by the *Guinness Book of World Records* as the smallest park on Planet Earth.

Actually, the colorful tale behind Mill Ends' creation begins with a hole in the ground on a median strip which was apparently meant for a traffic light or streetlight. Neither was installed, and a local journalist, Dick Fagan, apparently grew tired of looking at the void from his office window, so he planted his own greenery and pronounced it a park. Dedicated in 1948, the park became official in 1976.

MILL ENDS PARK

WHAT The only leprechaun colony west of Ireland

WHERE SW Naito Pkwy. at Taylor St., Portland, OR

COST None

NOTEWORTHY Portland also boasts one of the biggest urban forests in the nation. Forest Park covers more than 5,100 acres and contains more than eighty miles of roads, lanes, and trails.

Billed as a colony for leprechauns (whose leader Fagan claimed only he could see), Mill Ends has remained ever since. Over the years, a tiny swimming pool, statues and even a small Ferris wheel have graced the park's 452 square

Who says a park has to be big to be enjoyable? Certainly not the good folks of Portland, Oregon. Credit: Courtesy Portland Parks & Recreation

inches, as have concerts and picnics. It was such a local favorite that construction on its street didn't eliminate the park, which was temporarily relocated and then brought back.

There is a bit of non-leprechaun-related drama from time to time. In 2011, members of the Occupy movement even held a flash mob at the park, with one arrest made. Two years later, the park's sole tree was stolen. Another was promptly planted, since, as a spokesman for the parks department noted, someone had "to ensure the leprechauns had shade." In an oddly polite act by the vandals, the original stolen tree was mysteriously returned to the site shortly thereafter.

I guess you really don't want to anger leprechauns.

"Mill Ends" was the name of Fagan's newspaper column.

53

A MISNAMED MALADY

Why was one of the world's deadliest pandemics named after a country with which it had no connection?

There is still a great deal we don't know about the origin of the infamous Spanish flu, though there is one fact where everyone finds common ground. It didn't start in Spain.

That takes us to Haskell County in southwest Kansas. This unassuming bit of Midwestern real estate may not have many claims to fame but, according to modern research, it might have one to infamy. It may have been ground zero for a plague that would kill tens of millions and change world history.

The year 1918 was indeed a miserable time to be a human being. At least three of the Four Horsemen of the Apocalypse were riding roughshod across land and sea. But worse even than the ongoing First World War was a new and incredibly lethal strain of influenza that left a swath of mortality planetwide, easily outstripping the total of combat deaths and altering the course of the war.

Some of the earliest cases are still believed to have appeared in what is today Ft. Riley, Kansas, where troops began to contract the illness. Researcher John M. Barry has traced a possible origin even further, with the pandemic perhaps emerging in Haskell County, where a local physician reported people with a very nasty illness not long before soldiers began taking sick at the post 300 miles east. Soon, some of these men would ship out to Europe while

---

There was one place where the Spanish flu was never called that—Spain. Spaniards named the malady after the French.

Many of the graves in this American cemetery in France were from the flu that killed millions worldwide. Many scientists believe the "Spanish" flu began in America's heartland. Credit: National Museum of the U.S. Navy via Flickr under public domain

A BUG'S BEGINNINGS

WHAT The epicenter of an epidemic

WHERE Haskell County, KS, (probably)

COST 20-100 million deaths

NOTEWORTHY Frank Buckles, the last American "doughboy" to see World War I service in Europe, died in 2011 at age 110.

carrying a vicious microscopic killer that would fell more people than any army.

So why did the world eventually name this dread ailment after the Spanish? The answer is perception, propaganda, politics, and the press. Spain was among the few nations not at war that year. That meant it lacked the special restrictions on media that kept depressing stories—such as terrifying mass sicknesses—out of the news. Without censorship, information about early cases emerged in Spain before they did elsewhere.

As for the origin, nothing is for certain, of course. A wide range of theories place Patient Zero anywhere from Britain to China.

But Kansas remains the prime suspect. The misnamed Spanish flu was probably made right here in the good ol' USA.

54

THE UNSEEN WALL

Why are dozens of American cities bounded by nearly invisible wires representing a spiritual border?

You probably never notice it, but it's there. It crosses sidewalks, spans backyards, passes over highways. And if you live in one of many major metropolitan areas in the United States, you probably regularly cross this little-known demarcation of Secret America without even realizing it. It is a thin wire representing a unique spiritual border called an *eruv*.

The *eruv* is actually a creation of Jewish religious law, known as *halacha*, and derives specifically from prohibitions against performing work on the Sabbath. But the concept of "work" doesn't just include going to one's job. Even simple activities like carrying an object across a room can be considered a type of work and hence are forbidden for many observant Jews from sundown on Friday until sundown on Saturday.

Obviously, this can create practical difficulties, so Judaic law allows for certain forms of "carrying" within private spaces. How does one delineate a private space? According to *halacha*, a physical wall is required, but the wall can be represented by a simple wire. That's why Jewish communities will frequently organize an *eruv*, a wire that creates a continuous unbroken cordon, often enclosing significant sectors of major cities. Frequently hung from utility poles and lampposts, the border is thin—often fishing line is used—and intended to be unobtrusive. An *eruv* may also sometimes make use of existing wiring,

---

In 1970, only about ten eruvim were thought to exist on the continent, but the number has climbed rapidly since then.

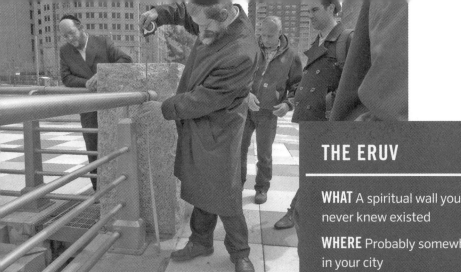

Measurements are taken for the Manhattan eruv. Eruvim exist in many cities, and you may pass through them every day without even knowing their spiritual importance to the Jewish community. Credit: Richard McBee/The Manhattan Eruv

THE ERUV

WHAT A spiritual wall you never knew existed

WHERE Probably somewhere in your city

COST Free

NOTEWORTHY Since its creation, the 18-mile long Manhattan *eruv* has been continuously in operation—despite periodic assault by everything from Macy's parade inflatables to Superstorm Sandy.

fences, walls, bridges, and similar objects to surround a given area. Arrangements are often made with local utilities and private landowners to create the *eruv*.

Despite this, an *eruv* is still no small undertaking. Every single line—miles and miles of it—must be inspected every single week, since a break anywhere would put those depending on it in violation of Jewish law. In fact, the Manhattan *eruv* alone is said to cost $100,000 annually to maintain. Some cities even run special phone numbers that Jews can call to make sure the *eruv* is unbroken each week. In 2015, Rabbi Adam Mintz, co-president of the Manhattan *eruv,* estimated that as many as 200 such borders may be in operation in cities across North America.

55 THE FAST AND THE FELONIOUS

How was one of America's favorite pastimes invented from criminal activity, and where can I drive a real race car?

Stock car racing is as American as Mom's apple pie. But unlike Mom's signature dessert, NASCAR signed an $8.2 billion television deal in 2013. The big-name drivers and their finely tuned machines have quite an audience.

Still, not everyone knows that some of the field's earliest figures had a good reason motivating their need for speed. They had cops chasing them.

Officially created in the late 1940s, the sport has roots going back to the days of bootlegging, when fast cars and daring drivers were tools of the trade for evading the authorities with profitable payloads of backyard beverages. Alcohol smuggling was first done to circumvent Prohibition and later to avoid paying taxes on the cargo.

Daniel Pierce, author of *Real NASCAR: White Lightning, Red Clay and Big Bill France*, said he was surprised to find that professional racing's connection to illicit spirits was everything the urban legends promised, saying, "The more research I did, the more liquor I found." He called it "foundational" to the sport. Even NASCAR's website confirmed in a 2012 article that the history of the enterprise

Junior Johnson was officially pardoned by President Ronald Reagan in 1985 for a three-decade-old moonshining rap, restoring his right to vote.

Going fast is a normal part of life in racing, but in the early days of NASCAR, the drivers sometimes found that the red flashing lights of the law in the rearview mirror provided a fine incentive to exceed the speed limit. The wild days of illegal hooch may be gone, but the Richard Petty Driving Experience at Daytona International Speedway can allow you to tear around the oval just like the pros. Credit: Courtesy of Daytona International Speedway

DAYTONA INTERNATIONAL SPEEDWAY

WHAT NASCAR's roots

WHERE 1801 W International Speedway Blvd., Daytona Beach, FL

COST Varies

NOTEWORTHY The first NASCAR race ever was won by Red Byron driving a Ford.

is "soaked to the very tips in moonshine." One of its most famous drivers, Junior Johnson, was also a notable participant in the business of running home brew.

Anyway, NASCAR's official—and completely legal—birth took place in Daytona Beach, Florida, and the Daytona International Speedway is a great stop for automotively inclined fans of Secret America. If you've ever wanted to experience the thrill of racing for yourself, you can time your visit to coincide with a running of the "Richard Petty Driving Experience." For as little as $135, you can ride shotgun for three laps around the track at speeds exceeding 160 m.p.h. Three other packages, ranging from $549 to $2,199, can put you in the driver's seat with professional instruction so you can take the checkered flag yourself.

56 THE MORNING OF TWO SUNRISES

Can I stand at the spot where the first nuclear bomb in history detonated?

Historic spots are vital because they give us a window on our beginnings, but the American Southwest houses a place where humanity got a truly chilling vision of our possible end. That vision came into unmistakably sharp focus just before dawn on the morning of July 16, 1945, when man's genius harnessed the hidden power of physics to unleash nineteen kilotons of hell upon Earth and forever convert a scrubby patch of New Mexican desert into an important part of Secret America.

The Trinity Test, as it was called, was a rousing success. The first atomic weapon ever used on Planet Earth had lived up to its billing. Exploding with the force of more than 20,000 tons of TNT, the blast was hot enough to melt sand at ground zero and created a new mineral, a radioactive glass called trinitite, some of which is still visible at the site today.

And, yes, you can visit the exact spot where humans introduced hot weapons to the Cold War. The birthplace of nukes is open the first Saturdays of April and October.

THE TRINITY SITE

WHAT A place where history is measured with a Geiger counter

WHERE Off U.S. Route 380 in Socorro County, NM

COST Free

PRO TIP There are no tours per se. Inquire with the Alamogordo Chamber of Commerce about joining their special visitors convoy to the site if you prefer to go with a group.

Just before dawn on an unassuming summer's morning in 1945, you would not have wanted to be standing where this marker now sits. Credit: White Sands Missile Range via Flickr

If two days a year seems strict, remember that the original event was even more exclusive, being something of a top-secret affair. Of course, there were certain obvious logistical challenges to keeping a seven-and-a-half-mile-wide mushroom cloud secret. At the time, the military told locals it was a munitions accident. Anyway, those privileged enough to be at the site got quite a show. One observer said he could feel the heat like an open oven door despite being ten miles away. Another compared it to the sun, which would crest the horizon just minutes after the test.

"We saw two sunrises," he said.

Big as it was, the Trinity Test released only a fraction of the energy of modern atomic bombs. The largest nuke ever detonated was Russia's Tsar Bomba, which yielded fifty megatons—more than 3,000 times the Hiroshima blast thought to have killed as many as 166,000 people.

"NOBODY SHOT ME"

Where is the execution wall from Chicago's St. Valentine's Day Massacre?

In the United States, there is a point at which yesterday's moral outrages become tomorrow's pieces of treasured Americana. And for a certain infamous garage wall against which seven men met their deaths at the hands of fellow mobsters one grisly St. Valentine's Day, that point has come and gone. But for those who want to see those bullet-riddled bricks (yes, the holes are still there), don't look in the Windy City. Instead, the neon glitz of Las Vegas awaits you.

The present owner of this stretch of murderous masonry is the Mob Museum in Nevada. In fact, the wall has been remarkably well-traveled since the 1929 incident. After a stint as an antiques warehouse, the building along Chicago's N. Clark Street where the killings took place was eventually torn down in the late 1960s, and several hundred of the bricks were saved from the scrap pile by a nightclub owner in Canada, where they eventually ended up as a backdrop for urinals at his Vancouver establishment.

Surprisingly, when the bricks came up for sale in 1996, Chicago had zero interest in this morbid but remarkable piece of Secret America. In fact, the then-president of the city's Chamber of Commerce said he would only favor buying the bricks for the express purpose of keeping them out of town. Notably, Chicago's antipathy toward the

---

The Mob Museum also contains such artifacts as Benjamin "Bugsy" Siegel's sunglasses, the old Nevada gas chamber chair and a ticket to the "Black Sox" fixed 1919 World Series.

Las Vegas, not Chicago, is the current home for the wall against which Al Capone's men gunned down their enemies. Credit: Courtesy of the Mob Museum

less-than-attractive relic of history can be seen by its lack of any acknowledgment for the spot where those members of the Moran gang met their end. The site of the former garage at 2122 N. Clark is now an unmarked grassy lot and parking area next to a nursing facility. Reportedly, it does still attract the occasional tourist, however.

As for the principals involved in the St. Valentine's Day Massacre, none fared very well. George "Bugs" Moran's gang was decimated, and his organization never recovered. Al Capone, widely believed to have ordered the hit, lost some of his benign public image as a shocked citizenry demanded reform. He would soon be in jail himself for tax troubles.

At least six of the men gunned down that day were dead by the time police arrived. Ironically, Moran, the target of the hit, wasn't among them. He'd apparently been late to the meeting. The sole survivor, a badly wounded Frank Gusenberg, didn't last long, but he kept the gangland honor code of silence to the end when police at the scene asked who had shot him.

"Nobody shot me," he reportedly said before succumbing to more than a dozen bullet wounds.

58 THE RICHEST HILL ON EARTH

Where can you visit a toxic lake that kills geese—and might help cure diseases?

Sitting on the outskirts of Butte, nestled in the mountains of Big Sky Country, is one of Montana's more interesting lakes. It is so interesting, in fact, that a special viewing platform has been erected, and visitors are charged just to see it.

But don't go kicking off your shoes just yet. "Viewing" is about all this body of water is good for. The more than forty billion gallons that reside in it aren't very conducive to a swim.

It is ironic that the Berkeley Pit began as a hill. Known as "the richest hill on Earth" for its generous quantities of ore, it became a fine spot for open pit mining of copper, which helped fuel Butte's growth. According to *The Washington Post*, the mine produced almost 300 million tons of copper from the mid-1950s until its closure.

THE BERKELEY PIT

WHAT A big hole full of toxic water

WHERE Along Continental Dr., Butte, MT

COST $2

NOTEWORTHY The PH level of the pit is about 2.5–3.0 which makes it about as acidic as vinegar or a cola drink.

But the prosperity had a cost and—after the mining stopped in 1982—water began to fill the void, eventually reaching a thousand feet deep and becoming infused with everything from cadmium to aluminum. For years, the pit was so heavily laced with metals that the company could acquire about 400,000 pounds of copper a month using a special process to "mine" *the actual water itself*.

Anyway, the mix of chemicals in the pit has, at times, made for some pretty colors on the lake's surface.

The richest hill is now a deep lake filled with some particularly unpleasant things floating in it.
Credit: Robert Ashworth via Flickr under Creative Commons 2.0

What's less pretty is the water's effect on unsuspecting fowl who make the mistake of stopping to rest there during migration. Those who stay too long never leave. In response, those who oversee the pit, now an EPA Superfund site, have initiated a program that includes everything from spotlights to noisemakers to people firing off guns to try and scare away birds.

Unfortunately, even that doesn't always work, and in 2016 a massive flock overwhelmed such efforts and left thousands of snow geese dead.

But, beyond making it a tourist destination, some are trying to harness the Berkeley Pit's contamination for positive ends. In the 1990s, medical researchers began to study the unusual properties of bacterial organisms found in the pit's toxic environs in hopes that they might be used to treat illnesses in the future. That anything can live there at all may be a surprise to some.

But, as they say, sometimes life is the pits.

The quantity of copper obtained from the Berkeley Pit could have created a four-inch-thick, four-lane-wide highway stretching from Butte to Salt Lake City, more than 400 miles away.

59 "CONTINUE, PLEASE"

Where did one of the world's most disturbing psychology experiments take place?

Linsly-Chittenden Hall may look like any Romanesque building on the stately Yale campus—architectural majesty in the dry air of academia.

But for the volunteers who reported there to take part in a dull-sounding experiment on teaching and learning in the summer of 1961, Linsly-Chittenden was about to turn into a bizarre house of horrors, one complete with screams of pain, switches to inflict agony, and a deeply disturbing window into the moral reasoning abilities of the human mind. However, these innocent, unsuspecting volunteers weren't going to be tortured.

They were going to be the torturers.

The rather unsettling part of Secret America housed at Linsly-Chittenden is called the Milgram Obedience Experiments, and it was the brainchild of Stanley Milgram, a professor at the school who wanted to answer the question of just how far individuals would go to obey an authority figure. To that end, volunteers were recruited to be seated in front of a board of switches representing ever-increasing electrical shocks.

A shill employed by Milgram in a different room posed as another volunteer. He was read various questions that he intentionally answered incorrectly, at which point a man in a lab coat leading the experiment told the volunteer at the panel to administer a shock that grew in intensity with each wrong response. Eventually, the shocks elicited shrieks of pain from the other room, as well as begging. The highest shocks elicited no sound at all—as though the subject were unconscious or possibly dead. When the participant at the board objected or wavered, the man in the lab coat

Linsly-Chittenden Hall has many stories to tell, but Milgram's controversial work there may be among its most significant tales. Credit: Michael Marsland/Yale University

LINSLY-CHITTENDEN HALL

WHAT A dark corner of the human psyche

WHERE Yale University, New Haven, CT

COST Your sense that it can't happen here

NOTEWORTHY Milgram was also a key player in the "small world experiment" which later became the basis for the concept of *Six Degrees of Separation* and pop culture fads like the Kevin Bacon game.

calmly issued a statement like "Continue, please" or "The experiment requires you to continue."

Of course, no real torture took place. No shocks were really administered and the board was phony. The true experiment had nothing to do with learning and was actually designed to test compliance. Would average Americans simply obey orders as the Nazis had famously said they were doing during their trials at Nuremberg?

Its findings were jarring. Nearly two-thirds of participants in the initial experiment completed the series of "shocks" despite screams, despite calls for mercy, despite even the suggestive silence indicating they'd evidently tortured and perhaps killed someone they'd barely met because someone else they'd barely met had instructed them to do so.

For some, the cognitive dissonance was not an easy process. A witness described one volunteer as "a mature and initially poised businessman" who sat down at the board "smiling and confident."

"Within twenty minutes he was reduced to a twitching, stuttering wreck who was rapidly approaching a point of nervous collapse," said the observer. "He constantly pulled on his earlobe and twisted his hands. At one point, he pushed his fist into his forehead and muttered, 'Oh, God, let's stop it.'"

But the man, like so many others, completed the experiment, pulling all the switches simply because an authority figure in a lab coat said that that was what he was supposed to do.

Milgram actually conducted many versions of the experiment to control for a number of factors, and he found that small changes could make big differences. Replacing the person in the lab coat with an "ordinary" individual sharply curtailed compliance rates. Perhaps tellingly, one of

---

The Zimbardo Prison Experiment at Stanford University in 1971 was another controversial effort. It created a mock "prison" in which some participants were designated "guards" and others "prisoners." Designed to last two weeks, it was shut down in six days due to the increasingly sadistic behavior of the "guards."

the biggest reductions in obedience occurred when others present—also shills of Milgram—began defying the orders of the authority figure. When subjects witnessed others saying no, their own rates of compliance dropped to just 10 percent.

Credit: Michael Marsland/Yale University

Other researchers criticized Milgram's ethics, saying that his subjects were misled and could have suffered psychological trauma from the incident. Moreover, not everyone feels the experiment truly proved what it advertised. Gina Perry, author of *Behind the Shock Machine: The Untold Story of the Notorious Milgram Psychology Experiments*, wrote in *Discover* magazine that Milgram's experimenter did not always adhere to the prearranged script and used other means of comforting or bullying participants into continuing. Moreover, she said that evidence suggests some subjects may have suspected the whole thing was a *Candid Camera*-style hoax.

Still, whatever its flaws and ethical concerns, the experiment remains a classic of psychology that raises questions of how the mind operates in situations where we should know what to do but an authority figure says differently.

As one participant said later, "The thought of quitting . . . never occurred to me. Just to say: 'You know what? I'm walking out of here'—which I could have done. It was like being in a situation that you never thought you would be in, not really being able to think clearly."

MAN OF THE PEOPLE

When did Jerry Springer run a major American city, and why does he do a weekly podcast at a Kentucky coffeehouse?

One thing no one can take away from Jerry Springer is a track record of success. Once called the "grandfather of trash TV," Springer doesn't really shy away from the title. If he didn't invent the genre, he certainly took it to brash new heights with such high-minded episodes as "I'm Happy I Cut Off My Own Legs" and "I Married a Horse."

But before heading a freak show featuring everything from midget Klansmen to countless cheating lovers, the king of daytime talk ran something much bigger—an entire American city.

Jerry Springer was once mayor of Cincinnati, Ohio.

Born to Jewish refugees from Nazi-occupied Europe, the young Democrat initially found a home in politics and was considered quite an up-and-comer on the city council, a man with a populist touch. He joined local garbage men for a day of collecting trash, passed his weekends driving the city's neighborhoods to listen to residents, and once spent a night in jail just so he could hear the problems of arrestees. By 1977, he was sworn in as mayor.

But that's where politics ended and Springer found himself entering media as a TV reporter. That local news

---

Springer's political career would have been limited regardless. He was born in Britain and, as such, is not eligible to run for president under the U.S. Constitution.

Just across the Ohio River from Cincinnati, the Folk School Coffee Parlor boasts friendly faces, tasty food, and a unique podcast with one very well-known mayor-turned-talk show host. Credit: David Baugher

FOLK SCHOOL COFFEE PARLOR

WHAT Jerry Springer's unexpected roots

WHERE 332 Elm St., Ludlow, KY

COST None

NOTEWORTHY Cincinnati's original name was Losantiville.

gig turned national by 1991, and *The Jerry Springer Show* came to life.

Before anyone is too hard on the ex-mayor for his questionable "contributions" to American pop culture, it should be pointed out that his signature TV program began with a more sober tone. Its initial incarnation featured serious guests as well as political and policy topics. But sagging ratings in the mid-1990s prompted more provocative programs. The wilder the guests got, the bigger the audience became.

So if we don't like Springer's three-ring circus, who do we really have to blame? Like any good politician, he was just keeping in touch with the desires of the common man.

Anyway, Springer still stops by the Cincinnati area and records a Tuesday podcast at the eclectic Folk School Coffee Parlor in Ludlow, Kentucky, covering everything from liberal politics to folk music. The podcast has no connection to the sort of topics found on his TV show. You can even reserve a seat to be in the live audience for it if you wish.

61 FROZEN DEAD GUY DAYS

How did a chilled corpse in Colorado become the center of a town's annual celebration?

Despite being the town's most famous resident, Bredo Morstoel never really got to know the good people of Nederland, Colorado. But that's not surprising. After all, he never started living there until after he died.

But Morstoel (also sometimes rendered Morstol), is now the center of this Rocky Mountain town's biggest annual festival. According to the *Boulder Daily Camera,* the story starts in the early 1990s, when a Norwegian family arrived in Nederland with their grandfather, who had passed away in 1989 but had been kept cryogenically frozen in hopes that he could eventually be revived at some future date.

Unfortunately, when Morstoel's presence on the premises was discovered, the authorities were less than enthusiastic about it and the town passed an ordinance against the keeping of frozen corpses.

Thankfully, however, "Grandpa Bredo," as he's affectionately known, was—quite literally—grandfathered in. Moreover, the town now celebrates their frigid citizen with "Frozen Dead Guy Days." Reminiscent of Mexico's "Day of the Dead" holiday, the event has a somewhat macabre feel, including such events as coffin races and a parade of themed and decorated hearses. The 2017 iteration even included a Frozen T-shirt Contest, a Frozen

---

Every month, Bredo Morstoel is packed with another 1,500 pounds of dry ice to keep him at –60 F.

Top: If you can't enjoy a good coffin race, just what can you enjoy? It's a question that rarely arises outside Nederland, Colorado. Credit: Andrew Wyatt with permission for use by Frozen Dead Guy Days

FROZEN DEAD GUY DAYS

WHAT Colorado's coolest resident

WHERE Nederland, CO

COST $10 for access to the music tents and $20 for the opening "Blue Ball" as of 2017, but entry fees vary for different events. No word yet on 2018 fees.

NOTEWORTHY At various times, tours of Bredo's chilly shed have been offered to interested parties, including at least one psychic who confirmed that Bredo is on the other side, where he is "doing fine."

Dead Poets Slam, and a Brain Freeze Contest, which involves the rapid consumption of frozen slushies and sounds like far more fun to watch than to participate in.

The event's owner was quoted in the local paper as saying that she loves the coffin races.

"It's funny," she said. "People are stumbling over coffins that fall apart. It's super fun, everyone really just enjoying themselves."

Perhaps Nederland's signature event is a bit of an acquired taste.

Anyhow, the festival, held every March, is within driving distance of Denver.

62 PERSONIFICATION OF A NATION

Was there ever a real Uncle Sam?

Some think of Uncle Sam as a being a bit like Santa Claus or the Easter Bunny—nothing more than a fictional personification created by pop culture and given his appearance only at the hands of a sketch artist.

But that's not quite true. There actually was a real Uncle Sam, and his origins are as old as the nation itself. Was he a politician? A statesman? A philosopher? A general?

Nope.

Born a decade before independence, Samuel Wilson made his trade in the meat industry.

So, how did a meat packer become the symbol for an entire nation?

By supplying its military with meat, of course. An army travels on its stomach, after all. Known to some locals as Uncle Sam, the initials of his nickname happened to match the stamps on his government-bound product. Soldiers started noting that the letters "U.S." might stand for Uncle Sam, and the idea gained fame via a newspaper account.

Of course, the imagery that would eventually take hold with the public did have a bit of help from the world

---

Cartoonist Thomas Nast wasn't the first to use a donkey to represent Democrats and an elephant to represent Republicans, but he popularized the concepts so much in the 1870s that he might as well have invented the association.

Yes, there was once a real Uncle Sam, and he rests in this New York cemetery.
Credit: Ron Cogswell via Flickr under Creative Commons 2.0

of fiction. Sam gained his beard from highly influential cartoonist Thomas Nast in the mid-19th century. But it was World War I that truly solidified Uncle Sam in the mind's eye of the populace. The famous "I want you for the U.S. Army" poster featuring a somewhat more demanding version of the figure—with an accusatory pointing finger and stern, guilt-inducing stare—was introduced by artist James Montgomery Flagg, who was also responsible for Sam's trademark star-girdled top hat.

As for the real Sam Wilson, like all mortal men, he proved less ageless than the iconic imagery he bequeathed to the country. He passed away in 1854.

Today, two towns can lay some claim to the real Uncle Sam. One is Troy, New York, where Wilson is buried and which was recognized by the U.S. Congress as his home. The other is Arlington, Massachusetts, where Wilson was born and where a statue still stands recognizing the man who has become as much associated with the United States as any human being could be.

Yet, so very few know his real name.

63 NO HOLIER PLACE

How did one officer's insult to a deceased foe become regarded as a great honor by the fallen man's family?

Much of what the American public knows about African American contributions to combat during the Civil War derives from Hollywood—in particular, the 1989 film *Glory*, which told of the 54th Massachusetts Regiment—an all-black contingent of the army. The movie gets many facts right.

Denzel Washington's character is a case in point. His actions at the climax of the film mirror those of a real soldier, William Carney, who did indeed grab the colors from a dying flag-bearer.

But unlike the character, Carney survived the battle. In fact, the wounded former slave wouldn't let go of the flag even as he crawled from the field, and still had it when he got to the hospital, proudly telling fellow soldiers that the emblem had never touched the ground.

Decades later, he became the earliest African American to earn the Medal of Honor.

There is one other scene in *Glory* that deserves explanation. After the battle at Fort Wagner, the lifeless body of Col. Robert Gould Shaw, the 54th's white commander, is shown being dumped into a pit with his men. This really did happen. A Confederate general buried him with the black soldiers as a sign of disrespect.

While the site of the oceanside charge by the 54th Massachusetts no longer exists, you can still see nearby Fort Sumter, where the first shots were fired in the War between the States. Credit: Fort Sumter National Monument

Ironically, it was regarded as an honor by Shaw's parents, who were grateful for the man's "insult" to their son.

"We can imagine no holier place than that in which he lies," said Shaw's father, "among his brave and devoted followers, nor wish for him better company—what a body-guard he has!"

Wagner has been reclaimed by the sea. But nearby Fort Sumter is a great place to learn about the war. If you are further north, a monument still commemorates both Shaw and the 54th in Boston, Massachusetts and an elementary school in New Bedford is named after Carney.

In the closing days of the war, even the Confederacy began using black soldiers, a move opposed by one reluctant Southern general who noted that "if slaves will make good soldiers our whole theory of slavery is wrong. . . ." He turned out to be right about being wrong.

Where can you listen in on messages meant for spies?

Almost everyone has the occasional private fantasy about the espionage game. Fast cars. Attractive women. Webs of intrigue. Who wouldn't love James Bond to drop by for one of his signature shaken martinis?

Of course we know that the real work of the super-secret universe of operatives and intel is far outside the realm of the common man.

But the surprising truth is that you can indeed crack open a small window on the cloistered world of cloak-and-dagger activities and, in doing so, you can marvel at a mystery that has fascinated ham radio operators for decades.

Welcome to perhaps the most secret part of Secret America—the shadowy domain of the numbers station.

Numbers stations create odd broadcasts on certain frequencies of the shortwave band that have been picked up worldwide going back decades. Some feature unique noises. Others involve a female or child reading repetitive strings of numbers, words, or letters. Attention signals, mysterious sequences of tones or short pieces of music, can sometimes be heard. For a time, one station merely emitted a constant buzzing sound. Some are intermittent, but many transmit messages at certain set times. These broadcasters never identify themselves or their origin or respond to inquiries.

Exactly what these bizarre transmissions mean no one quite knows, but virtually everyone understands that

NUMBERS STATIONS

WHAT Spies unlike us

WHERE On the air tonight

COST Free to listen

NOTEWORTHY The 2013 John Cusack spy thriller *The Numbers Station* used the mysterious broadcasters as part of its plot.

With a shortwave radio or just an internet connection, you can listen to espionage in action. All those monotone numbers, strange tones, and random words mean something to someone, but only the intended listener knows exactly what. Credit: Pixabay

what they are hearing isn't meant for civilian ears. Experts believe it to be espionage related. Someone somewhere is furtively listening and decoding these cryptic messages with a special key.

Why broadcast messages for spies on airwaves anyone can listen to? Because without the key, no one else can understand and—even in the electronic age—the best way to ensure that your message is untraceable back to the receiver is through general broadcast.

The strange stations have developed intense followings among non-spies, who find the mystery fascinating. Some are even given colorful names like "The Lincolnshire Poacher," "The Sexy Lady," or "Bulgarian Betty." Entire websites have sprung up on the internet complete with livestreamed audio and schedules to allow for easy listening even if you don't have a radio.

Numbers stations are believed to be heavily active in Russia, China, Taiwan, both Koreas, Poland, and the Middle East, though many suspect that U.S. and British stations have mostly ceased broadcasts, according to an article in the *Daily Beast*.

65 THE ULTIMATE TREEHOUSE

Can you make a log house using only a single log?

The idea of the log cabin has held a certain rustic romance for Americans ever since we all found out that Abraham Lincoln grew up in one. What could connote the idea of the simple life better than a humble structure made from dozens of logs?

How about a one made with just one log?

As bizarre as it might seem, it is possible, and for some wonderful folks in picturesque northern California, it is a daily reality. That's because they run the "One Log House," a remarkable single-piece structure hewn painstakingly from a solitary forty-two-ton chunk of redwood. Construction owed more to sculpting than to traditional building techniques, as workers burrowed a seven-foot by thirty-two-foot room out of the trunk, which was itself more than two millennia old. In fact, management says the amount of lumber chipped out of the tree-turned-building could have constructed a five-bedroom house. Notably, two men completed the project in just eight months.

Made just after World War II, the rounded inside is lighted and furnished motorhome-style with dining, living, and bedding areas, making the cozy space into what can only be called the ultimate treehouse.

The tallest redwood tree clocks in at 379 feet. That's more than twice the height of the Statue of Liberty from toe to torch tip.

The One Log House in Northern California is the sort of treehouse that most kids could only dream of making.
Credit: Courtesy of One Log House

THE ONE LOG HOUSE

WHAT Solid lumber construction

WHERE 705 U.S. Route 101 near Garberville, CA

COST Inquire on-site

PRO TIP This area is surrounded by numerous state parks, conservation areas, and national forests and is just 120 miles south of Redwood National Park, which is also on Route 101.

Since 1999, the house, which is (somewhat) mobile, has resided just inside Humboldt County adjacent to Richardson Grove State Park. It is associated with an espresso and gift shop that includes information, photos, and tools related to logging practices. Best of all, it advertises that necessity for any true tourist locale on the great American road—clean restrooms.

66 A TILTING POINT IN HISTORY

How was the Leaning Tower of Pisa saved by a twenty-three-year-old American?

Obviously, the Leaning Tower of Pisa does not reside in America, but the reason this legendary edifice still stands does live here. His name is Leon Weckstein, and the bizarre tale of how the tower's fate was possibly decided by a single twenty-three-year-old GI may be one of the least-known stories of World War II.

It all began as Americans progressed up the Italian peninsula in the summer of 1944. Weckstein was the young sergeant ordered by his commander to scout out the situation in the town of Pisa. In particular, he was supposed to assess whether the Nazis were using the famous tilted structure as a vantage point to observe or direct fire.

"Sergeant," he later recalled the colonel telling him, "if you see anything that looks suspicious up there, any . . . damned . . . enemy . . . movement at all . . . don't . . . hesitate! Call in fire to blast the thing to kingdom come!"

Taking along a radioman, Weckstein did his job and peered at the tower to see any evidence of an enemy presence, steeling himself to utter a single sentence back to HQ that would have leveled the 14th century structure. Yet, he found himself struck

THE LEANING TOWER OF NILES

WHAT A replica of the Leaning Tower of Pisa

WHERE 6300 Touhy Ave., Niles, IL

COST Proposed repair work to the Niles tower was estimated in 2016 to cost over half-a-million dollars

NOTEWORTHY The Leaning Tower of Niles was built in 1934.

Okay, so this isn't the tower that Leon Weckstein saved but if you want to see it, Illinois is closer than Italy. Credit: Lawrence Kestenbaum via Flickr under Creative Commons 2.0

by its beauty as well as distracted by waves of heat rising from the ground, making it impossible to tell if anyone was there or not. He admits he was "just about to blow the thing to smithereens." Still, he paused. Weckstein never did give the order. He also never found out for sure if the Germans were using the facility.

Meanwhile, the moment having passed, Weckstein's superiors radioed that they'd decided the planet's most famous construction mistake would get a reprieve.

Weckstein, who authored *Through My Eyes: 91st Infantry Division in the Italian Campaign, 1942–45,* would never forget that day. Neither would the city whose landmark he didn't blow up. Pisa honored him with a medallion in 2000.

Incidentally, even if you can't afford an Italian vacation, you can still see a replica of the iconic tower that Weckstein saved right here in the good old US of A. The Leaning Tower of Niles, a half-sized version of the building, resides in Niles, Illinois, a suburb of the Windy City.

As for Weckstein, he still wonders if the Germans were using the Leaning Tower as an outpost.

"I've had fifty years to think about it, and I'm pretty sure they were," he told *The Guardian* newspaper in 2000.

Initially, the Leaning Tower of Pisa tilted north, but continuing construction changed its slant to the south.

SOCK IT TO ME

Where was the first American football game, and where does the word "soccer" come from?

Let's face it. The word "football" makes absolutely no sense when applied as most Americans use it. It is a game concerned primarily with carrying and throwing a ball—things you can't do with your feet. Meanwhile, Americans (along with Canadians and Australians) have taken the kick-intensive sport the rest of the world properly calls football and rechristened it "soccer."

To investigate why, we have to go back to the origins of American collegiate football, which began with a game played on November 6, 1869. Of course, no modern fan would recognize what took place on the field that day in New Jersey between Rutgers and Princeton. There was no gridiron, no passing, no carrying, no officiating, no helmets, and very few firm rules. Players basically kicked, smacked or headed a ball in the general direction of a goal. It looked less like the NFL and more like a cross between soccer and an outdoor bar fight. At one point, things got so chaotic that a Rutgers player accidentally scored a goal for Princeton, and a collision by two players caused the makeshift bleachers to collapse. A contemporary account described "headlong running, wild shouting and frantic kicking," or—in the words of a *Princeton Magazine* retrospective—"a coin toss and then bedlam" consisting of "grit, muscle and an unholy amount of testosterone."

Athlete Walter Camp is credited as having invented most of the rules of American football, including downs and the quarterback position.

The College Avenue Gymnasium now occupies the site where that first chaotic game of football—or whatever it was— got underway well over a century ago.
Credit: Rutgers, The State University of New Jersey

RUTGERS UNIVERSITY

WHAT The birth of collegiate football—or possibly soccer— or both

WHERE 130 College Ave., former site of College Field, New Brunswick, NJ

COST None

NOTEWORTHY The NCAA was created at the urging of President Theodore Roosevelt—largely to combat the epidemic of injuries and deaths in the increasingly brutal sport of college football.

Whatever it was, it was generally called football, a sport that began to diverge between a more rugby-like, hands-based game and a less violent kicking-oriented version in the late 19th century.

According to a 2014 article in *The Atlantic*, rugby took on the moniker "rugger," as opposed to its more foot-centered cousin called "association football," which was truncated into "soccer" from the "soc" in "association."

Eventually, that word fell out of favor in Britain but gained usage in nations like the United States and Australia, where other sports were being called "football." Within a few years, rules were written, and by the early 20th century, forward passes were allowed. That's how a game of carrying and throwing became known as football, while a game of using your feet to move the ball got called something else.

68 THE MOST FAMOUS MARQUEE

Why did the iconic "Hollywood" sign originally say something else, and why was it never intended to be permanent?

Even in a city defined by famous people and places, the giant letters spelling out "Hollywood" above the nation's movie capital are an iconic site—as enduring as the film classics produced in one of the most culturally influential places on Planet Earth.

But it may surprise many to learn that this sign was never supposed to be iconic or enduring. In fact, it wasn't supposed to last more than a couple of years. And it was never meant to promote the city of Hollywood.

Actually, it was an advertising stunt. Originally, the letters, assumed to be temporary, said "Hollywoodland," the name of some new residential development up in the hills way back in 1923. After that, they just sort of stayed for a couple of decades until local officials wanted

---

In 1932, the Hollywood sign became a symbol of the movie business's crueler side when despondent actress Peg Entwistle left a brief suicide note before throwing herself from the top of the "H." Some say the twenty-four-year-old still haunts the hillside.

Inexorably tied to movie magic, this onetime temporary advertising sign has become an icon recognized around the planet. Credit: Pixabay

them torn down. But more nostalgic heads prevailed and the city decided to keep the landmark—with the last four letters removed.

By the late 1970s, however, decay and neglect had left the marker falling to pieces. A quarter-million-dollar fundraising effort was launched among Tinseltown luminaries to bring back the glory days of the big white letters. The work was a success.

Today, most would never guess that this piece of treasured Americana is essentially a repurposed billboard.

69 A VISITOR FROM THE SKY PEOPLE

Where can I see the heart of an ancient planet?

Today, the solar system has only eight recognized planets. That's down from nine due to poor Pluto's demotion a few years back. Yet in its wild early days, our celestial neighborhood was a much more crowded place. The eight big ones we know today are just the survivors. But we can also get a clue as to some of the other early contenders for planethood via a trip to New York City, where a massive 15-ton chunk of worn iron sits proudly on display in the American Museum of Natural History.

This is no ordinary meteorite. This was once at the heart of a forming planet.

Unfortunately, the early solar system was a violent locale, and this young orb was among the casualties, due to a collision with other large objects. Had trajectories been just a bit different, we might still have nine planets today, with this piece of iron helping to form the core of one of our near neighbors. Then again, if we hadn't been so lucky, perhaps a lump of proto-Earth's core would be sitting on display in an alien museum somewhere being viewed by inhabitants of the would-be planet now in New York.

In any event, this heavenly visitor apparently arrived in Oregon's Willamette Valley millennia ago, which accounts for its label, "The Willamette Meteorite." But it actually had a far earlier name. The object was called Tomanowos and

---

Only about 5 percent of meteorites that impact Earth are made of iron like Tomanowos.

It is a big universe and there were many protoplanets. Earth was one of the lucky ones to make the cut. Credit: Pixabay

the Clackamas tribe believes it was an honored representative of the Sky People. Today, the Confederated Tribes of Grand Ronde continue to treat the meteorite with great respect and regularly visit it to sing prayers and perform ceremonial rites. In fact, their special relationship to Tomanowos has been codified via a specific agreement that posits recognition of the tribe's connection to it and stipulates that control of it will revert to the tribe should the museum ever stop displaying it.

Notably, the museum has an entire section—the Arthur Ross Hall of Meteorites—that is devoted to space rocks. That includes part of one of the more famous ones, which slammed into—and through—the trunk of a red 1980 Malibu owned by eighteen-year-old Michelle Knapp in 1992. Among the many calls the Knapps received in the wake of publicity over the incident was one from their insurance company to let them know that their policy didn't cover impacts from space. Purchased by private collectors, the battered car would go on to be far more well traveled after its demise than it had been during its useful life, having been sent on a world tour from Japan to Germany.

ROCK 'N' TOLL

Who is the only person confirmed to have been struck by a meteor?

In *Julius Caesar*, Shakespeare famously wrote that the fault is in ourselves, not in our stars.

But the Bard might have been more charitable if he'd met Sylacauga, Alabama, housewife Ann Hodges on November 30, 1954, when she was hit with something that would nearly kill her, present her with opportunities for fame, prompt a court fight, and ultimately ruin her life. It was that day that Hodges became the only human ever positively confirmed to be struck by a shooting star.

The thirty-four-year-old was napping when the meteorite punched through her roof and slammed into her thigh after ricocheting through the room.

At first, Cold War paranoia gripped the town, with some suspecting the meteorite was some kind of Soviet spy device but once authorities confirmed that the celestial event was not the vanguard of a nefarious Bolshevik plot, media came calling. According to a *Mental Floss* article, Hodges appeared on game shows and even in *LIFE* magazine. But the rock's value brought up the question of to whom it belonged. Hodges's landlady, as the owner of the building, laid a claim. Hodges countered that God had intended the rock for her. "After all, it hit me!" she said.

THE HODGES METEORITE

WHAT A Rock of Misfortune

WHERE 6th Ave. and Capstone Dr., Tuscaloosa, AL

COST $2 for adults

NOTEWORTHY A widely filmed meteorite that exploded over Russia in 2013 was said to have injured as many as 1,200 people, mostly due to broken glass from shattered windows or other objects.

From the day it first fell into her life, this 8.5-pound stony meteorite brought nothing but trouble to an Alabama housewife, but it did assure her a place in history as the only confirmed person struck by a rock from space. Credit: Alabama Museum of Natural History

Hodges gained title to the stone, but the interest of a fickle public had cooled. No one cared. Ultimately, the rock Hodges had fought so hard to keep was used as a doorstop in her home. Worn down by court fights and publicity, Hodges had a nervous breakdown and separated from her spouse, with both saying they wished the meteorite had never come into their lives. She died at just fifty-two.

The rock can still be seen at the Alabama Museum of Natural History. A *National Geographic* article quoted the institution's director, noting a sad epilogue.

"The Hodges were just simple country people," he said, "and I really think that all the attention was her downfall."

According to Stephen A. Nelson, a professor who calculates such things, your odds of being killed by a localized meteorite strike are 1 in 1.6 million. That's actually far better than the 1 in 195 million odds of hitting the lottery jackpot in Powerball.

71 MEETING AT THE TRIPOINT

Why is everything you know about the Mason-Dixon Line wrong?

From cultural interest articles to cooking shows, people have come to talk so casually about the Mason-Dixon Line and its historical role as a cross-country Civil War divider between north and south that it can be easy to forget a few key facts about this oft-mentioned border.

First, it had nothing to do with dividing north from south. Second, it isn't cross-country. Third, it has no connection to the Civil War.

Yep. Pretty much everything you know about the Mason-Dixon Line is complete rubbish.

In fact, the real line surveyed by Charles Mason and Jeremiah Dixon has its roots in a long-standing border dispute between the colonies of Pennsylvania, Maryland, and Delaware, which began back in the 17th century and was so complicated that it didn't get fully worked out until 1921 and still left Marylanders with one of the more oddly

---

Daniel Emmett, the fellow who created the iconic song "[I Wish I Was in] Dixie," which became the preeminent Southern rallying cry during the Civil War, was a Yankee. It was penned in New York. He came to regret his invention, saying bitterly that if he'd known its future use, "I will be damned if I'd have written it."

The Tri-State Trail weaves back and forth across the Delaware–Pennsylvania state line a couple of times before hitting the tripoint with Maryland. But you still won't have to do as much walking as Mason and Dixon. Credit: April Abel/ Delaware State Parks

shaped states in the union, with a bizarre one-hundred-mile panhandle that's only two miles across at its narrowest point.

According to a fine history by the University of Delaware's John Mackenzie, the problems began, as many things do, with a royal proclamation in which King Charles II gifted a rather extensive chunk of land to William Penn in 1681. Its border with neighboring Maryland was marked as the 40th parallel, an arrangement that was hampered somewhat by the fact that no one knew precisely where that was. Philadelphia's old downtown actually lies a bit to the south of that line, which means that Pennsylvania's largest

Verdant fields await along your journey past the real Mason-Dixon Line.
Credit: April Abel/Delaware State Parks

city was technically founded in what should have been Maryland.

But by the 1730s, when folks noticed that the future Keystone State was actually a squatter on large stretches of its southern neighbor, it was too late to do much about it. After almost four decades of sporadic and pointless violence failed to resolve the issue, the authorities in England got tired of all the nonsense. Both sides were pressured into a compromise border, and Mason and Dixon were hired to figure out exactly where it was.

The pair had nothing to do with the Civil War, which wouldn't even be fought for nearly a century, and their now-famous line never extended west of Pennsylvania. Moreover, the line never touches the Potomac and remains NORTH of Washington, D.C. The three states it divides all remained with the Union.

Still, the "Mason-Dixon Line" is used as shorthand for a barrier between north and south. It's even believed that

The trail may twist and turn, but on both sides of the imaginary Mason-Dixon Line, you'll remain in the North. Credit: April Abel/Delaware State Parks

the phrase "Dixie" for the Confederacy may derive from Dixon's name.

As for the dynamic duo themselves, they were a one-hit wonder, and the Mason-Dixon Line was their only project together. Neither of the two men who demarcated America's most enduring boundary were American, by the way. Both were British.

Anyway, you can still see some of the pair's handiwork by visiting the Maryland–Delaware–Pennsylvania tripoint stone marker, which can be accessed from a four-mile loop trail. Parking is available in either Delaware or Pennsylvania, but the Keystone State has a shorter walk.

72

RAGE WITH RELISH

Why is this restaurant famous for verbally abusing customers?

There are plenty of themed restaurants out there—some of them with pretty wacky motifs. But it is likely that none give quite the experience of one Chicago hot dog stand where raunchiness and vitriol flow as freely as the mustard.

The Wiener's Circle in Lincoln Park has become something of a Chicago tradition over the years. Yes, people like the signature char-dogs and the fries. But the real draw to this unusual eatery is the verbal interplay between patrons and staff, which frequently involves language as unpalatable to sensitive ears as hot dogs at a fancy soiree. This is not a place to take the kids. In fact, it has become nationally famous for its frequently drunk-late night clientele, who exchange insults with the workers.

While some of the daytime interactions are more pleasant, the late-night and weekend crowd, often coming from nearby clubs and bars, has a rowdier history. Francis Lam, a writer for Salon.com, in 2010 called his evening experience there "a face-twisting orgy of aggression," where the social contract wasn't merely broken but "set on

---

The Wiener's Circle was purchased by new management in 2015 and one of the new owners said patrons would see "some changes over time" but also noted "We're very aware of what makes the place special" and that it would "still look and feel like the restaurant they know and love."

After all these years, The Wiener's Circle remains a landmark in the Windy City.
Credit: Nicolas Henderson via Flickr under Creative Commons 2.0

THE WIENER'S CIRCLE

WHAT Service without a smile

WHERE 2622 N Clark St., Chicago, IL

COST Yelp lists the price range at under $10

NOTEWORTHY During the 2016 election, the Wiener's Circle provided its own form of tasteful political commentary by offering a special "Trump footlong," which turned out to be a three-inch hot dog.

fire and waved in your face." Swear words, including racial epithets, were common during his visit, as was the "chocolate shake," a tradition in which an employee would expose her chest if customers provided enough money.

"I hear the tips are great," wrote Lam in an article entitled "The Most Depressing Hot Dog Stand in America." "I hate this place."

Indeed, the verbal jousting isn't for everyone. Catherine Price included the establishment in her book *101 Places Not to See Before You Die,* along with such classics as "The Great Pacific Garbage Patch" and "The Inside of a Spotted Hyena's Birth Canal."

Still, while it is clearly not for everyone, this rude corner of Secret America has a developed a pretty loyal following, both for the food and the . . . well . . . entertainment of customers and employees letting loose from the normal rules of human social interchange. One 2017 Yelp reviewer complimented the fare as "pretty good," adding, "One of the employees made a girl cry so that was funny."

73

LIFE ON THE LINE

Where can you see a stage performance in another country from a seat in the United States?

The United States and Canada have always enjoyed a certain degree of cultural closeness. For many, the border has seemed less an international barrier and more a charming formality.

Nowhere is that truer than in Derby Line, Vermont. It is here, where the Green Mountain State meets the Land of the Maple Leaf, that people have long felt a kinship with their friends across town in Stanstead, Quebec. This is where foreigners are neighbors.

The Haskell Free Library and Opera House certainly hews to that ethos. It is one of the few buildings anywhere with an international border running through it. In the opera house portion, most of the seating is in the United States but the stage is in Canada, so you quite literally can see a play or performance in another nation from the comfort of a seat in America.

Dedicated to merchant Carlos Haskell, the structure's placement was entirely intentional back when it was built in 1904. The library, which features such un-library-ish touches as fireplaces and sofas, has most of its books on the Quebec side of the border, while the entrance is on the U.S. side. The spot has been a huge tourist attraction for the town.

The entire U.S.–Canadian land border is marked by a twenty-foot-wide clear-cut strip through the forest to promote visibility for security reasons.

The stately Haskell Free Library and Opera House stands as a testament to America's longstanding friendship with its Canadian neighbors. Credit: John Fox/Courtesy of the Haskell Free Library

Unfortunately, the post-9/11 world has reached everywhere—even this quiet corner of northern Vermont—and border enforcement agents have been seen cropping up more often while tourism has slackened a bit. Being smack dab on the border can create logistical complications for even the most ordinary aspects of life. For instance, Canadian visitors to the library are allowed to walk to the Haskell's American entrance, but driving to its parking lot requires a visit to customs.

Moreover, while visitors can travel freely within the building, they must return to their country of origin upon departure.

The security precautions have not been popular, though they aren't entirely unjustified. In 2011, one visitor to the Haskell allegedly attempted to smuggle guns across the border.

Still, the increased security presence and the corresponding loss of innocence hasn't been a pleasant experience for many townsfolk.

"It's just not fun anymore," one resident glumly told the *Toronto Star* that year.

74

A LETTER OF INTENT

Why do people misspell Pittsburgh?

Every town has its oddities, but the silent "H" tacked incongruously to the end of Pennsylvania's second-largest city has frustrated takers of geography exams for generations. Even nearby West Pittsburg doesn't use the extra letter.

But it might surprise many to know that the issue roiled the waters of both the local and federal governments for decades. From the printer's error in 1816 that caused the legislature to misname the city to the world's most famous baseball collectible, a Honus Wagner card that depicts him playing for "Pittsburg," to a United States Geographic Board of Names decision in 1891, everyone seems to want to strip the city of its beloved "H". To this very day, even the town's train station has the misspelled version etched into its rotunda.

To comprehend the confusion, one must understand why the "H" is there in the first place. According to a 2000 article by James Van Trump in *QED Renaissance*, the term "burgh" is actually the Scottish descendant of "borough," an older and mostly archaic type of administrative division (though some places like New York City still use it).

"Burg" is a German relative of the term. But the Scottish version "burgh" is pronounced like "borough" (or "burrow"). That is why you not only see a lot of –burgs,

---

According to a 2015 survey commissioned by King Digital Entertainment, the most difficult city to spell in the United States was Meeteetsee, Wyoming.

With or without its elusive "h", Pittsburgh's enduring heritage as a river city can be seen through its bridge-heavy skyline. Credit: Pixabay

PITTSBURG(H)

WHAT A city of three rivers and one "H"

WHERE Pittsburgh, PA

COST None

NOTEWORTHY According to a 2006 study, Pittsburgh had more bridges than any city in the world, including Venice, Italy. Twenty-nine of the town's 446 spans are over its three major rivers.

-bergs, and -burghs in the United States, but a number of -boros as well. It is no accident that John Forbes, the fellow usually credited with labeling "Pittsburgh," was Scottish. He used the "H," although he spelled it "Pittsbourgh," which was probably pronounced like "Pittsboro."

Anyway, by 1891, the federal government, possibly during a fit of boredom, decided to standardize American place names. In addition to taking on such weighty matters as hyphen usage and "center" versus "centre," the powers-that-be decreed that "-boroughs" should become "-boros" and that any "burgh" should have its "H" amputated for simplicity's sake.

That explains the train station carving and Honus Wagner's uniform. For two decades, Pittsburgh actually was Pittsburg, a change affecting everything from sports teams to newspapers.

But the locals never liked the idea, and by 1911, the bureaucrats in Washington, D.C., finally capitulated and Pittsburgh got its "H" back, where it remains to this day.

75

HAMBURGER HELPER

Where was fast food invented?

Today, the corner of N. Main and 1st Streets in Wichita, Kansas, could pass for pretty much any intersection in any American town from coast to coast. But appearances can be deceiving. This seemingly ordinary spot in this most ordinary of towns saw the rise of something that would forever change how Americans—and the world—eat.

This is the spot where fast food was born.

When most people think fast food, they think McDonald's, but while the Golden Arches were certainly an early—and fantastically successful—entry in the market, they didn't invent the concept. Nor did Burger King, Wendy's, or Jack in the Box.

The honor of pioneering the great American burger joint goes to White Castle. In fact, to a large degree, it pioneered the hamburger. No, they didn't invent the meat patty, but they did popularize it by rehabilitating the image of ground beef in an era when it was viewed as low-class or even unsanitary.

Owners Edgar "Waldo" Billy Ingram and J. Walter Anderson put together a "clean" look to their restaurants, from their bright-sounding name to the crisp steel and gleaming enamel to the uniforms that bespoke hygienic professionalism.

The signature five-hole design of White Castle's slider patty was introduced in 1947 in order to help the burger cook faster and end up more flavorful.

Both the name and logo of White Castle still reflect its roots, inspired partly by the castle-like design of an historic water tower in Chicago. Credit: David Baugher

THE CORNER WHERE FAST FOOD BEGAN

WHAT The burgers you love to buy by the sack

WHERE 201 N Main St., Wichita, KS

COST Still cheap

PRO TIP The lot of the old White Castle is now occupied by a bank.

Nearly two decades before the first McDonald's opened, White Castle was debuting the assembly line methods for food preparation and the step-by-step standardization that would come to define the industry by ensuring a quick, tasty, cheaply produced product that rarely varied regardless of who was preparing it that day. It was a fast meal for average folks at a reasonable price, and within a few years of its opening in 1921, White Castles were spreading across the Midwest. They even created their own company to supply paper hats for workers. By some accounts, Anderson effectively invented the hamburger bun.

In any event, the burger had, for better or worse, come to assume its dominance over American diets.

76

THE AMAZON QUEEN OF CALIFORNIA

Does the name of our most populous state descend from Arabic?

State names are a hodgepodge of words with British, French, Spanish, and Native American roots. As Idaho proves, some of them were simply made up from thin air.

But of all the states, California may have the most bizarre potential etymology. It may in fact be derived from Arabic, and the backstory behind its labeling takes us on a convoluted centuries-long journey through Moorish conquests of Iberia, Christian crusades, and a mythical Amazonian queen before concluding in the syrupy pages of an ancient romance novel.

The strange tale begins with a fellow by the name of García Ordoñez de Montalvo, a 16th-century Spaniard who penned *Las Sergas del Muy Esforzado Caballero Esplandián, Hijo del Excelente Rey Amadis de Gaula*, or The *Exploits of the Very Powerful Cavalier Esplandián, Son of the Excellent King Amadis of Gaul*. One can only assume that short, catchy titles were not Montalvo's forte as a writer.

The Spaniard's swashbuckling book introduced California, a blissful utopian isle situated near Eden and populated by a race of beautiful warrior women. (Well, to be more precise, it was a blissful utopia *if* you were a beautiful warrior woman. Male visitors were apparently killed on sight and fed to mythical griffins, so first dates were presumably rare.)

In any case, California's name appears related to that of its leader, Queen Calafia, and Calafia's name itself appears to be a female derivation of "Caliph," a Muslim leadership role. In fact, the queen and her women-in-arms—all of whom were dark-skinned—spend the novel helping Islamic Ottomans battle Christians during the crusades, an apt

CALAFIA AVENUE

WHAT A real novel, a fictional queen, and the land they may have named

WHERE Oakland, CA

COST None

NOTEWORTHY Streets in various other California cities including Glendale and Temecula bear Calafia's name as well.

The California branch of the grizzly bear family is sadly only to be found on its flag. The now-extinct animals were heavily hunted and by the early 20th Century were just as non-existent as Calafia's Amazonian army. Credit: Pixabay

topic in Montalvo's homeland, since it had been ruled by Moors for generations. California may indeed have been named after a character from the 16th-century equivalent of a Danielle Steele novel.

It should be noted, of course, that opinion is far from unanimous on whether Montalvo's work named California. Competing theories include Native American words for "high hill" or Catalan variations on the words for "hot oven."

But Montalvo and Calafia's mythical realm remain the prevailing speculation for the origin of the state's label. California may indeed be the only state whose name has Arabic roots. One can still see this legacy today with the name of Calafia Avenue in Oakland, California, near I-580.

According to *Mental Floss*, Florida is the oldest European-bestowed state name in the United States, having been named by Juan Ponce de León in 1513.

77

STAYING STICKY

Why is a Seattle wall coated in used chewing gum?

Henry Ward Beecher once said that every artist dips his brush into his own soul. But in at least one Seattle alleyway, the media for great art requires less of what's in the soul and more of what's in the mouth.

Welcome to the Gum Wall, one of the odder tourist attractions in the nation and a gooey testament that some things can be beautiful and amazingly icky all at the same time. Like so many other worthy human endeavors, this massive mosaic of America's chewable guilty pleasures began with tiny acts of thoughtless vandalism. Queued theater patrons smacked their used gobs of gum on the masonry outside the Market Theater. Soon, enough of the sticky stuff was there to encourage others. Management initially fought against the gum goliath, but after a time, it became clear that frequent scrapings were a losing battle. Sometime after it began in the early 1990s, the powers-that-be mostly adopted an "if you can't beat 'em, join 'em" approach, and today the wall is considered a tourist attraction.

There is still some effort to control the build-up. In 2015, the bricks were painstakingly cleaned with crews spending 130 hours to pull two decades of accumulated gummage off the wall, netting more than 2,300 pounds of chewable art media.

THE GUM WALL

WHAT Chewable art

WHERE Pike's Place Market, Seattle, WA

COST A pack of gum

PRO TIP Be prepared for a bit of an odor—described by one CNN article as "fruity." As one Yelp contributor put it, "It is a wall of gum. It smells exactly how you would expect a wall of gum to smell."

This book is in black-and-white but if it were in color, this photo would be just as beautiful as it is gross. Credit: David Fulmer via Flickr under Creative Commons 2.0

"The gum will be thrown away, officials say," read a part of *The Seattle Times* article that one would hope might have gone without saying.

Anyway, gum began returning the very next day. Some of the earliest additions were Eiffel Tower-shaped peace signs to mourn the Paris terrorist attacks that had just occurred. According to Yelp reviews, the wall has begun to resume its former glory. Most agree that the brightly hued wall presents an excellent, if very disgusting, photo opportunity. It is that rare kind of participatory artwork that requires both a noble creative spirit and plenty of hand sanitizer. Some have even begun adhering their business cards to the surface as a form of advertising. After all, if you can't trust professional services from someone whose name you found on a wall of gum, who can you trust?

However you view it, the Gum Wall remains the stickiest part of Secret America.

Seattle isn't the only competitor in the gum-based tourism industry. San Luis Obispo, California, has a "Bubblegum Alley" based on much the same concept.

78

HARVEY'S HARD DAY

What was the best single-game pitching performance in Major League history?

Just a few dozen yards outside present-day Miller Park in Milwaukee is a Little League field, and on one of the nearby walkways for that field is an outline of home plate as it was when Milwaukee County Stadium stood on this spot. From there, you can stare sixty feet and six inches out into the distance to contemplate the strange ironies that can accompany great achievement.

That's because on May 26, 1959, it was here that a thirty-three-year-old southpaw for the Pittsburgh Pirates received a remarkably painful object lesson in the capricious nature of what it means to be the best. It was here that hurler Harvey Haddix exercised complete dominion over this plate, pitching what was unquestionably the best game of baseball ever tossed from a Major League mound. And it was here also that Haddix somehow lost that game.

The perfect game is baseball's rarest gem. Yet Haddix, despite sporting the less-than-fearsome nickname "the Kitten," didn't just manage perfection through nine innings. With the contest still scoreless, he continued to

In 1970, Dock Ellis, another Pirates hurler pitched a notable no-hitter but it wasn't pretty. Ellis walked eight batters during that first game of a doubleheader. He later revealed that he'd been on LSD and only recalled bits and pieces of the contest.

Miller Park now sits near the old site of Milwaukee County Stadium where Haddix pitched his epic loss. Home plate for the old stadium can be found at Helfaer Field, a youth baseball field near the parking area. Credit: Jeramey Jannene via Flickr under Creative Commons 2.0

HELFAER FIELD

WHAT The greatest game ever pitched

WHERE Outside Miller Park, Milwaukee, WI

COST Just parking

PRO TIP Don't miss the nearby parking area, where you can find a brick-ringed plaque in the asphalt marking the place where Hank Aaron's famous 755th home run landed.

retire batters in extra innings. The 10th, the 11th, the 12th—Haddix sent thirty-six men down in perfect order.

But his team didn't score a run, and in the 13th, an error finally allowed a base runner. An RBI base hit ended the hurler's wizardry two batters later. The run was unearned.

Even grizzled baseball observers were stunned. So was Haddix, who walked the streets of the city until dawn trying to wrap his head around what had just happened.

But that wasn't the end of the story. In 1991, more than three decades after Haddix's game, baseball delivered the final twist of the knife, noting that a pitcher must keep a team hitless even during extra innings to earn a true no-no. They retroactively revoked the poor pitcher's no-hitter.

He died three years later. His achievement is marked on his tombstone. Perhaps it was Lew Burdette, Haddix's opponent that night, who best summed up the evening.

"I have to be the greatest pitcher who ever pitched," mused Burdette, "because I beat the guy who pitched the greatest game ever pitched."

79 FLYING BLIND

Why is America dotted with mysterious cement arrows?

It sits off the side of a sparsely traveled country road in Indiana about halfway between Cincinnati and Indianapolis. Cracked and broken, the concrete has seen better days. But the shape is unmistakable. This is an arrow. Nearly 70 feet in length, it beckons enigmatically toward an unknown goal as though part of a treasure hunt for giants. But this oddity isn't alone. Just a few miles to the northwest in neighboring Shelby County, another arrow appears, pointing in the same direction as its cousin. Harder to see from ground level, they are easy to pick out from above on Google Maps.

And there are still more of them. The brush of the New Mexican desert, a yard in suburban Minnesota, a remote outpost in Utah, near a crossroads in South Carolina. From Connecticut to California,

THE TRANSCONTINENTAL AIRWAY SYSTEM

WHAT Guides to low-tech flying

WHERE Dozens of states, particularly west of the Rocky Mountains

COST None

PRO TIP "I just wanted to see a big arrow" is a bad excuse for trespassing, so try and remember that a lot of these things are on someone else's private property now.

Three of the lighted beacon towers are still used in Montana, maintained for "nostalgic aviators," according to the state's Department of Transportation.

Painted bright yellow, this concrete arrow at the Shelbyville Municipal Airport just southeast of Indianapolis helpfully points pilots in the right direction along the old air route between Cincinnati and Chicago. Credit: David Baugher

Georgia to Washington State, these bizarre markers are everywhere across the fruited plain.

What they are is an odd relic of a bygone time before radar and traffic control towers made flying the mundane activity it is today. They were part of an ingeniously simple navigational matrix called the Transcontinental Airway System. With the birth of airmail, early pilots needed methods to know where they were going at night. The solution was a series of illuminated towers that directed flyers, much like their maritime lighthouse companions did for boats. At the base of each tower was a brightly painted arrow pointing the way to . . . well, usually to another tower and another brightly painted arrow spaced out about every ten miles or so in between major cities.

Some of these arrows, a number of them with towers, still survive despite being disused by the 1940s. Left to the elements, they merely lay cracking in the sun, an abandoned part of Secret America made unnecessary not long after their introduction in the 1920s.

If you want to find them, more than 400 are thought to still exist, and plenty of websites can be your guide. You'll have better arrow-hunting luck west of the Rockies, though, where the antiquated navigational markers have survived in larger numbers.

80

GUIDING LIGHT

Where is the nation's oldest operating light bulb?

We live in a disposable age, and few products could be more emblematic of that than the humble incandescent light bulb. It may brighten our evenings, yet its short life span inevitably leaves us in the dark—usually teetering unsteadily on a chair to screw in a fresh one.

But that mundane chore is not something that the good folks at the Livermore-Pleasanton Fire Department in Livermore, California, need to worry about. Their bulb has been burning for well over a century and is in the *Guinness Book of World Records* for the feat.

The hand-blown bulb was donated to the station back in 1901 and has been lit since at least 1902, with its carbide filament burning continuously during that time, save for the odd power failure and its having been moved from one station to another. Parties have been hosted in the bulb's honor, and in 2001, it was even recognized by President George W. Bush as an "enduring symbol of the American spirit of invention." The Centennial Bulb, as it is known, has even entered the modern age by acquiring an email address, a Facebook page, and a webcam, which was set up to keep track of its every enthralling moment. All it needs now is a blog and couple of selfies.

The Livermore bulb isn't the only one that's burned for more than a century. The "Palace Bulb" at a Fort Worth, Texas, theater attained that mark in 2008.

A defiant symbol of quality workmanship in a disposable age, this little light bulb shines on, showing that even the most humble of household items can be built to last. Credit: Jay Galvin via Flickr under Creative Commons 2.0

THE CENTENNIAL BULB

WHAT Elderly electrical equipment

WHERE 4550 East Ave., Livermore, CA

COST None

PRO TIP The bulb does receive visitors, assuming any firefighters happen to be on-hand when you ring the doorbell. If not, you can see it through a special window.

Of course, the years have taken their toll on the old bulb. It now emits light at only about four watts, a fraction of its original brightness. Oddly, after being off for almost half a day in a power outage, the bulb briefly returned to its original 60-watt luminosity for several hours after being reactivated. No one knows the reason.

In any event, the superannuated bulb, which marked its one-millionth hour in 2015, is believed to be not just the oldest in the nation but also the oldest in the world, a reminder that harkens back to an age in which electrical lighting was still a cutting-edge innovation for the planet.

81

THE JAPANESE ATTACK ON OMAHA

What were balloon bombs, and what was their purpose?

Evidence of the battles of the Second World War are commonplace all over the planet. From the hallowed beaches of Normandy to the Eurasian steppes of Russia to the jungled islands of the Pacific, the war impacted much of the Earth.

But Omaha, Nebraska, would probably rank among the least likely places one might expect to see a memorial to a combat assault. Yet, the corner of 50th and Underwood contains just such a marker, noting the day in April 1945 when this suburban stretch of real estate came under attack by the Empire of Japan.

That attack came in the form of a balloon bomb, one of the more remarkable and least reported technological innovations of the war. The Japanese released about 9,000 hydrogen-filled balloons to drift slowly across the sea, carried aloft by the Pacific's westerly winds. Equipped not just with explosives, they also had barometers and a clever system of sandbags and hydrogen release valves that kept them from floating too high or too low on their journey. The Omaha bomb traveled some 6,000 miles, comparable to the range of today's ICBMs.

And that's how residents of Omaha came to witness explosives lighting the night sky that evening. A historic plaque marks the spot to this day.

Japanese balloon bombs have been found from Alaska to Michigan.

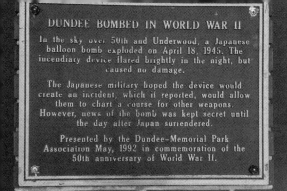

DUNDEE BOMBED IN WORLD WAR II

In the sky over 50th and Underwood, a Japanese balloon bomb exploded on April 18, 1945. The incendiary device flared brightly in the night, but caused no damage.

The Japanese military hoped the device would create an incident, which if reported, would allow them to chart a course for other weapons. However, news of the bomb was kept secret until the day after Japan surrendered.

Presented by the Dundee-Memorial Park Association May, 1992 in commemoration of the 50th anniversary of World War II.

This plaque immortalizes an attempted aerial assault on the nation's heartland that few realize even happened. But Japanese balloon bombs were a real phenomenon and even claimed lives in at least one incident. Credit: Molly Romero/Dundee-Memorial Park Association

THE BALLOON BOMB HISTORICAL MARKER

WHAT An innovative method of attack

WHERE 50th and Underwood, Omaha, NE

COST None

NOTEWORTHY Each balloon carried an explosive payload weighing more than thirty pounds.

Though little known, the Omaha incident wasn't as rare as one might think. More than 300 balloon bombs have been catalogued, and the truth is that no one knows for sure what happened to the remainder of them. Were they victims of capricious Pacific breezes? Or did they simply land peaceably, still lying in wait in some remote area of North America? These aren't just idle thoughts. In 2014, a Canadian forestry crew came upon one of the old devices, necessitating the use of navy bomb disposal technicians.

And while the Omaha bombing caused no damage, that wasn't always the case. A Washington State balloon took out the power lines to a weapons plant. Meanwhile, less than a month after the Omaha balloon, one of the explosive inflatables was found by pregnant Sunday school teacher Elyse Mitchell near an Oregon roadside.

"Look what I found, dear," she remarked to her husband.

They were her last words. Seconds later, Mitchell and five of her students gained the tragic distinction of becoming the sole bombing-related deaths recorded in the lower forty-eight contiguous states during World War II.

82 THE LONGEST ROAD TRIP

What famous team failed to play its first home game for more than four decades?

There is plenty of interesting trivia about the world-renowned Harlem Globetrotters. One of the most famous sports teams in the nation, they've also been immortalized as an iconic cultural institution, with on-court antics and a signature blend of sportsmanship and showmanship that is uniquely American.

But it might surprise many to learn that the Harlem Globetrotters weren't from Harlem. In fact, they didn't play a single game in the place whose name they bear until 1968—a forty-two-year road trip.

The team's real birthplace was in the Chicago area, where they became known as the Savoy Big Five before an early name change to their present moniker in 1927. That's when their first "road game" was played in Hinckley, Illinois. A sign in the town still marks the

THE GLOBETROTTERS' FIRST ROAD GAME

WHAT The Illinois birthplace of Harlem's most famous team

WHERE Near Hinckley-Big Rock High School, 700 East Lincoln Hwy. (U.S. 30), Hinckley, IL

COST None

NOTEWORTHY In 2015, Pope Francis was inducted as an honorary Harlem Globetrotter. He is the second pope to gain that title, joining John Paul II and such luminaries as Whoopi Goldberg and Henry Kissinger.

The Washington Generals were named after President Dwight Eisenhower, who was, of course, a former general.

It isn't Harlem but rather Hinckley, a small town in Illinois, that can claim the roots of the Globetrotter organization, as well as the four decade-long road trip that followed its inception there.
Credit: David Wilson via Flickr under Creative Commons

occasion. The name Harlem was adopted due to the team's African American roster.

Contrary to legend, the Trotters are capable of losing—even against their longtime archrival punching bags, the infamous Washington Generals. It is unclear exactly how many games the opposing squad actually won against their famous cousins. Some accounts say the Generals won as many as six while losing about 16,000 or so. But at least one 1971 win was particularly memorable. Like the proverbial hare facing a tortoise, the Trotters put so much effort into glitz that they lost track of the score. A last-minute surge put the game in overtime, but the Generals—at the time playing as the New Jersey Reds—sunk the winning basket, leaving the crowd in stunned silence.

"They looked at us like we killed Santa Claus," recalled coach Red Klotz.

The Trotters' owner even stormed into the locker room and yelled at Klotz that he was supposed to lose.

"No way," replied Klotz fresh from breaking a nearly 2,500-game losing streak, "And if you let your guard down, we'll get you again."

83

PLAYING WITH FISSION

Did a Michigan teen once build a backyard nuclear reactor out of household items?

In the early morning hours of August 31, 1994, police in Clinton Township, Michigan, on the outskirts of Detroit, answered a call about someone stealing tires. What they found instead was an evasive teenager, a sealed toolbox, and an eclectic collection of items, including strange cubes of powder encased in foil, mercury switches, vacuum tubes, fireworks, and various acids.

These cops—along with a dizzying number of state and federal agencies—had unwittingly stumbled into a truly surreal corner of Secret America. Their host on this journey was David Hahn, a most unusual adolescent, who had just spent the past couple of years attempting to build a nuclear reactor in a backyard shed using items like coffee filters, duct tape, and smoke detectors. Stunningly, he had managed to get far enough in the process to generate measurable radiation across much of his neighborhood.

Hahn had long enjoyed dangerous chemistry experiments, and in 1991 he'd earned an Eagle Scout merit badge for atomic energy by making a model of a reactor using a juice can. Now, he wanted to go further. Installing a Geiger counter on the dashboard of his car and making calls posing as a professor, he began a search for actual radioactive materials.

Eventually, he acquired them—radium from old glow-in-the-dark clock dials, americium from smoke detectors, thorium from certain types of gas lanterns, beryllium from a community college chemistry department, uranium from

According to Ars Technica, Hahn died of alcohol poisoning in 2016.

Ever wonder what your neighbors' most unusual hobbies are? For residents in one Michigan neighborhood, the answer to that question turned out to be as innovative as it was frightening. Credit: Pixabay

A BACKYARD NUCLEAR REACTOR

WHAT The China Syndrome next door

WHERE Clinton Township, MI

COST None

NOTEWORTHY In 2011, *Gizmodo* reported that the home of a Swedish man was raided and radioactive materials found after he attempted to split atoms in his kitchen.

naturally occurring ores he located, tritium from certain luminescent sporting goods.

While most of these things were relatively harmless by themselves, Hahn manipulated, purified, extracted, and combined large quantities of them into increasingly energetic materials until the seventeen-year-old eventually had a core that was—in his words—"radioactive as heck."

But by this point, according to an article in *Harper's Magazine* by author Ken Silverstein, the young man was reading radiation as far as five houses away. After his shed was raided, the EPA undertook a Superfund cleanup of the site, noting "an imminent and substantial endangerment to public health or welfare or the environment."

"These are conditions that regulatory agencies never envision," one state official told Silverstein in 1998. "It's simply presumed that the average person wouldn't have the technology or materials required to experiment in these areas."

Hahn told authorities that the whole thing was part of his effort to become an Eagle Scout.

Silverstein, the magazine's writer, would go on to author a book on Hahn entitled *The Radioactive Boy Scout.*

84

CARBONATION BUBBLE

Is there really a gigantic pool of liquid carbon beneath the Western United States?

I don't want to alarm anyone, but if you live in certain regions of twelve Western states, there is a good chance that you are presently sitting atop a massive lake of molten carbon the size of Mexico.

Mostly, when we think of geological activity out west, thoughts tend to center on the San Andreas Fault, the famous seismic zone responsible for San Francisco's 1906 and 1989 earthquakes. But while California's shakiness may impress us on a human timescale, its problems pale in comparison to potential issues further east. Beneath the feet of placidly grazing buffalo and happy tourists in Yellowstone National Park is the epicenter of a monster of epic proportions. It is the bubbling cauldron of a supervolcano. Supervolcanoes are much larger than the ones we periodically hear about on the news. Catastrophic blasts like those from Mount St. Helens or Mount Vesuvius are charmingly cute by comparison.

Supervolcano eruptions, however, are truly biblical in scope. Fortunately, they don't happen a lot. In fact, modern humans have never seen one occur.

But we certainly *know* they have occurred. In fact, that's why Yellowstone exists in the first place. The park's famous thermal features like Roaring Mountain and Old Faithful aren't powered by the National Park Service.

Yellowstone's biggest eruption, which happened 2.1 million years ago, released about 6,000 times as much lava as 1980's Mt. St. Helens blast.

The geysers in Yellowstone don't just spout up for your entertainment. They are fed by a very big and somewhat unsettling part of Secret America that lurks beneath this park's beautiful scenery. Credit: David Baugher

THE BIG, HOT LAKE

WHAT Lots o' lava

WHERE Under Yellowstone National Park

COST $30 for most private non-commercial vehicles

PRO TIP If you plan on more than one visit during the year, an annual pass to the park is $60.

They derive their boundless wellspring of steamy energy from deep underground. In 2015, scientists estimated that enough magma resides beneath Yellowstone to fill the Grand Canyon 11 times over.

If the Yellowstone supervolcano were to get ornery, it would be a pretty catastrophic event, possibly sending the earth into a "volcanic winter" due to the amount of ash involved. Notably, the last big Yellowstone eruption took place nearly 700,000 years ago and deposited ash as far away as eastern Mississippi.

The United States Geological Survey calls the possibility of such an eruption in the next few thousand years "exceedingly low." Just be aware that when you visit Yellowstone, you are in fact walking on one of Secret America's biggest time bombs. Fortunately, it has a very long fuse.

85 BOMBS AWAY!

What American city keeps a memorial in the town square to mark the time it was accidentally bombed by the U.S. military?

You probably haven't heard of Cimarron County. Besides the geographical oddity of being the sole county in America to border counties in five states, this rural outpost at the tip of the Oklahoma panhandle doesn't have many claims to fame.

But one of them is the mock bomb crater in the county seat of Boise City, complete with a model of a bomb. They mark the strange night this little hamlet came under attack from the United States military.

It all came about one quiet July evening in 1943 when a training mission went pretty remarkably awry. Aircraft from neighboring Texas zeroed in on what they believed to be the lights of a test target but which was in fact the Boise City Courthouse. The bombs were mostly filled with sand, but there were enough explosives to wake up a good portion of the townsfolk, who must have wondered how exactly their tiny village became a strategic target for the Axis Powers.

Fortunately, no one was hurt and even the courthouse remained standing.

"They did pretty darned good," the city attorney told *The Oklahoman* in 1990. "Although none of the bombs

BOISE CITY BOMB CRATER

WHAT A hole in the ground

WHERE 4 NE Square, Boise City, OK

COST None

NOTEWORTHY The Oklahoma Panhandle's origins come from the Missouri Compromise, which prohibited the further expansion of slavery north of Missouri's southern border—thus shaving about thirty-four miles off the top of the panhandle of Texas, a slave state.

The day after Independence Day, 1943, the fireworks were still going off in Boise City, Oklahoma, thanks to some errant flying by area military pilots. Credit: Courtesy Judy Broaddus

hit the courthouse, all of them were within ninety-three-feet."

Local officials even hoped to get some members of the B-17 crew to show up to 50th anniversary festivities, but contemporary media reports indicated that that was a tough prospect.

"We've done our best to locate these guys," the city attorney told the newspaper. "I guess they are a little reluctant."

He said that was unnecessary.

"No one around here is mad—anymore," he noted.

The iconic wailing sound of German Stuka divebombers you remember from every WWII movie was no Hollywood invention. It also wasn't engine noise. The Nazis intentionally fitted the planes with special air sirens so they would frighten people during dives.

How is this monument to veterans specially designed to be viewed on Veterans Day?

Most places in America honor the nation's armed forces, which have consistently been a beacon of unity even in divisive times.

Yet the memorial that honors them in Anthem, Arizona, displays unity in a whole new light—literally. In fact, it is designed to showcase that unity once every year—at 11:11 and 11 seconds in the morning on November 11—which, of course, is 11/11.

It is that exact moment when the sun is fully aligned to send its beams down through ovals in five consecutive pillars representing different branches of the United States military. When the light strikes the ground at that precise moment, it will illuminate a glass rendering of the Great Seal on the floor of the memorial.

The logistics involved in the marker weren't easy to achieve—or even to explain.

"When planning the geometry of the Anthem Veterans Memorial," said Jim Martin, the memorial's chief engineer, "it was clear that the static nature of the structure would require a fixed azimuth (the horizontal angle from astronomical north to the center of the sun on November 11 at 11:11 a.m. that creates the horizontal illumination of the

The date 11/11 wasn't chosen as Veterans Day for its catchy number scheme. It was the day the armistice took effect ending WWI in 1918. Hostilities ceased at 11 a.m. that day.

When the light aligns at 11:11 a.m. on 11/11, the image on the bricks glows in the rays of the sun, symbolizing the unity of our nation and the bravery of its heroes. Credit: view2az via Flickr under Creative Commons 2.0

THE ANTHEM VETERANS MEMORIAL

WHAT Where the sun spotlights heroes

WHERE 41703 N Gavilan Peak Pkwy., Anthem, AZ

COST None

PRO TIP The red pavers on the ground and the white memorial pillars represent two of the nation's three colors. The third is represented by the blue sky.

Great Seal) and a fixed altitude angle (the vertical angle for zenith, or horizon, to the center of the sun on November 11 at 11:11 a.m. that creates the vertical illumination of the Great Seal)."

Of course, due to the vagaries of calendars and celestial motion, lighting up the seal at precisely 11 seconds after the minute isn't really possible. The whole thing would have to be moved a tad each year to account for minor adjustments.

But Martin was quoted on the Anthem Community Council website as saying that it is accurate down to within a 24-second window.

That was good enough for the Arizona Historical Society, which has given it landmark status. It has also been honored by the Arizona chapter of the American Public Works Association and the American Consulting Engineers Companies for its innovative design.

Moreover, the memorial, which was dedicated on 11/11/11 (when else?) will be accurate for quite some time to come.

"We also checked the variance 500 years out," said Martin. "If the structure is still standing, it will work."

87

THE REAL RHODE ISLAND

How did America's smallest state acquire the name "island" when it isn't one?

It is a paradox that baffles young geography students from the time they first learn all the names of the states. Rhode Island isn't an island. It has never been an island, and it is very much connected to the mainland United States.

What is going on here?

Well, first of all, Rhode Island isn't actually named Rhode Island. The real name of our smallest state is Rhode Island and Providence Plantations. (Yes, you don't actually know the real name of one of our fifty states. It's kind of like when you found out Pluto wasn't a planet.) Anyway, "Rhode Island" is just a shortened version of the actual name, which no one uses because it is ludicrously long.

So where did the name come from? Actually, there really is a real island of Rhode Island, which is where the state got its moniker. The biggest island in Narragansett Bay, home to such towns as Portsmouth and Newport, is officially called Rhode Island, although at some point, many of the locals, in a probable attempt to avoid confusion, began reverting to its Indian name, Aquidneck Island, and that's what many call it today.

So, to sum up, everyone calls Rhode Island, the state, Rhode Island, even though that's not its real name and it is not really an island. Meanwhile, no one calls Rhode Island, the island, Rhode Island even though that is its real name and it is where the state acquired its name.

Rhode Island and Providence Plantations is the smallest state in the union but has the longest name.

Welcome to Rhode Island, which isn't an island and isn't really named Rhode Island. Credit: Taber Andrew Bain via Flickr under Creative Commons 2.0

RHODE ISLAND AND PROVIDENCE PLANTATIONS

WHAT The little state with the big name

WHERE Turn left at Connecticut

COST None

NOTEWORTHY Rhode Island's nickname, "The Ocean State" is well deserved. It has more than 400 miles of shoreline.

Incidentally, there was no fellow named "Rhode" for whom the island or the state is labeled. Both are said to derive their name, for some mysterious reason, from the Island of Rhodes, which is also actually an island but is in Greece. However, others say Rhode Island came from a Dutch explorer named Adrian Block who named Rhode Island (the island) Red Island, or Roodt Eylandt. But there isn't a lot of consensus on this point. In fact, both incompatible stories appear on different parts of Rhode Island's official state website.

88

KEEP ON TRUCKIN'

Where is the world's largest truck stop?

Feeling the pull of the open road is easy for any holiday traveler, but for truckers, the nation's interstates aren't paths to vacation destinations. They are just another day at the office, and it is these drivers that help keep the nation's lifeblood of cargo flowing.

Living out of a big rig means you need more from your rest stops than a snack bar and clean restrooms. That's where truck stops come in. These supersized gas station/restaurant combinations are a staple for many a weary traveler.

Still, even by the standards of truck stops, Iowa 80 is an achievement. Sometimes called a "truckers' Disneyland," this sprawling outpost in eastern Iowa is a virtual city all its own, serving some 5,000 customers every day with everything from a barber shop to a chiropractor on the premises. There's even a dentist, a custom embroidery and vinyl shop, a movie theater, and a pet wash for drivers who have Rover along for the ride. The main building is nearly 100,000 square feet. From the gift shop to the laundry facility to the workout room, if they haven't got it, you don't want it.

This family-owned locale had humble beginnings back in 1964 but has since undergone twenty-eight remodels and

---

In more than half a century in business, Iowa 80 has served more than 3 million cups of coffee and 18.2 million eggs.

What would a "Truckers' Disneyland" look like? With a visit to this haven of the open road in Iowa, you just might find out. Credit: Courtesy Iowa 80

IOWA 80

WHAT The mother of all truck stops

WHERE 755 W Iowa 80 Rd., Walcott, IA

COST Depends on what you buy

PRO TIP In addition to the chain restaurants on-site, the Iowa 80 Kitchen is open 24 hours and seats 300.

expansions and now boasts enough space for 900 tractor-trailers, 250 cars and twenty buses.

It has become a repository of trucker culture as well. The Iowa 80 Trucking Museum (with about ninety trucks on display) is on the premises and the facility plays host each July to the Walcott Truckers Jamboree, which was expected to attract about 44,000 people in 2017.

Needless to say, Iowa 80 is a twenty-four-hour, 365-day-a-year operation. Plus there is still room for further expansion. The entire campus is about 225 acres. Only about seventy-five have been developed.

And, of course, they do have clean restrooms. In fact, this mega-truck stop goes through about fifty-five miles of toilet paper each month.

89 THE SECRET LIFE OF NUTMEG

Why is Connecticut nicknamed after a spice not grown there?

Missouri is the Show Me State, Ohio is the Buckeye State, and West Virginia is forever the Mountaineer State. Every place has some claim to fame to stick on a license plate or a college sports team. Then there is Connecticut.

Unofficially, it is known as "The Nutmeg State." That might not be so bad. After all, everyone loves a good eggnog.

But nutmeg is a tropical tree, and much of the United States—outside a few sections of Florida and California—is ill-suited to its need for equatorial heat and stifling humidity. Certainly, Connecticut is about as far removed climatologically from the tree's native Indonesia as one could imagine. There just aren't many jungles encroaching on Hartford. Nutmeg isn't grown in the Nutmeg State.

Why the name?

Nutmeg may not have flourished here, but Yankee traders did, and apparently much imported nutmeg made its way from exotic foreign shores to Connecticut. Unfortunately, not all of those traders were necessarily honest. Rumor has it that wooden substitutes may have been swapped in for genuine nutmegs. Trying to spice up

The covering of nutmeg seeds can be used to make mace.

It may populate kitchen shelves here, but the most famous spice in Connecticut isn't grown there. Credit: Pixabay

THE NUTMEG STATE

WHAT A spice from afar

WHERE Connecticut

COST Check the seasonings shelf

NOTEWORTHY Nutmegs look a bit like walnuts and come from a type of evergreen tree.

your pumpkin pie with sawdust shavings probably made many a customer none too happy.

Still, some theorize that it was uneducated buyers rather than unscrupulous sellers who may have given the state's merchants a bad name. Those acquiring nutmegs may have not known that you have to actually grate them to make them of much use.

In any event, Connecticut residents continue to be known as "nutmeggers" despite the irony that the only examples of that spice in this state are found in the same little jars one sees everywhere else.

BIBLIOGRAPHY

1. **Car-free is Carefree:** "Fort Mackinac and The War of 1812" MHUGL. By Anthony Amato. Oct. 11, 2015. http://ss.sites.mtu.edu/mhugl/2015/10/11/fort-mackinac/; "Fort Mackinac History" Mackinac State Historic Parks. http://www.mackinacparks.com/more-info/history/individual-site-histories/fort-mackinac-history/; "Mackinac Island Loop (State Highway 185)" TrailLink. https://www.traillink.com/trail/mackinac-island-loop-(state-highway-185)/

2. **A Spiteful Spike:** "FAQ" National Park Service Golden Spike. https://www.nps.gov/gosp/faqs.htm; "Climbing the Promontory" Golden Spike National Historic Site, https://www.nps.gov/parkhistory/online_books/hh/40/hh40o.htm

3. **Armageddon in Wayne County:** "ID: F-70" North Carolina Highway Historical Marker, http://www.ncmarkers.com/Markers.aspx?MarkerId=F-70; "US Plane in 1961 'nuclear bomb near-miss'" BBC. Sept. 21, 2013. http://www.bbc.com/news/world-us-canada-24183879; "U.S. atomic bomb disaster narrowly averted in 1961; nuke almost exploded over N.C. by accident" CBS News. Sept 23, 2013. http://www.cbsnews.com/news/us-atomic-bomb-disaster-narrowly-averted-in-1961-nuke-almost-exploded-over-nc-by-accident/; "Nuclear Mishap – Wayne County, North Carolina" ExploreSouthernHistory.Com. http://www.exploresouthernhistory.com/nuclearnc.html; "Almost Armageddon" *Arkansas Democrat-Gazette,* Oct. 7, 2016. By Philip Martin.

4. **Right Angles in the Wrong Spot:** "Why the Four Corners Monument is in exactly the right place" National Geological Survey. May 15, 2009. By William Stone. https://www.ngs.noaa.gov/INFO/fourcorners.shtml; "The national monument that's in the wrong place" *Conde Nast Traveler.* July 1, 2013. By Ken Jennings. http://www.cntraveler.com/stories/2013-07-01/four-corners-monument-quadripoint-maphead-ken-jennings

5. **The King of Mattoon:** "The burger king and queen of Mattoon" *Illinois Times.* Nov. 20, 2003. By John Jermaine; "Mattoon's Burger King gets a new owner" *Journal Gazette & Times Courier.* Mar. 3, 2017. By Rob Stroud; "Today's special: Mattoon burger King gets new owners" *The News-Gazette.* Feb. 8, 2015. By Don Dodson; "Is Sarah Michelle Gellar really banned for life from McDonald's?" *Huffington Post.* Nov. 12, 2015. By Brian Cronin. http://www.huffingtonpost.com/brian-cronin/is-sarah-michelle-gellar-_b_8531828.html

6. **Headwear Hooliganism:** "The 1922 Straw Hat Riot was one of the weirdest crime sprees in American history" *Slate.* April 3, 2013. By Justin Peters. http://www.slate.com/blogs/crime/2013/04/03/straw_hat_riot_remembering_one_of_the_weirdest_crime_sprees_in_american.html; "Columbus Park" NYC Parks. https://www.nycgovparks.org/parks/columbus-park-m015/history; "The Straw Hat Riots of 1922" *Mental Floss.* By Mark Mancini. http://mentalfloss.com/article/61755/straw-hat-riots-1922; "The Great New York Police Riot 1857 and the Five Points Riot of New York 1857" The History Box. http://www.thehistorybox.com/ny_city/riots/sectionII/printerfriendly/nycity_riots_article2a.htm

7. **A True Tripleheader:** "Just because: June 26, 1944 – Dodger vs. Yankees vs. Giants" CBS Sports. June 18, 2013. By Dayn Perry. http://www.cbssports.com/mlb/news/just-because-june-26-1944--dodgers-vs-yankees-vs-giants/; "Three dimensional baseball" SABR Research Journals Archive. By William G. Nicholson. http://research.sabr.org/journals/three-dimensional-baseball; "In 1944, all three NY baseball teams faced off to support the war effort" *New York Daily News.* May 10, 2014. By Roger Rubin; "The LA Dodgers got their name from Brooklyn's deadly streetcars." *Gizmodo.* June 10, 2015. By Adam Clark Estes. http://gizmodo.com/the-la-dodgers-got-their-name-from-brooklyns-deadly-str-1687077696; "The First Baseball Game" State of New Jersey. http://www.state.nj.us/nj/about/baseball.html

8. **A Hairy History:** "Loose Cannons: 101 Myths, Mishaps and Misadventure of Military History" By Graeme Donald. Osprey Publishing. 2009, Goldfinch's Wig; "Events of April 18, 1775" The Old North Church. http://oldnorth.com/historic-site/the-events-of-april-18-1775/; 10 things you may not know about the Boston Tea Party. History.com. Dec. 14, 2012. By Christopher Klein. http://www.history.com/news/10-things-you-may-not-know-about-the-boston-tea-party

9. **The Center of Attention:** "How an internet mapping glitch turned a random Kansas farm into a digital hell." *Fusion.* April 10, 2016. By Kashmir Hill. http://fusion.net/story/287592/internet-mapping-glitch-kansas-farm/; "Kansas couple sues over internet glitch targeting their home." *The Wichita Eagle.* Aug. 8, 2016. By Oliver Morrison; "The Internet is now officially too big as IP addresses run out." NBC News. July 2, 2015. By Alex Johnson. http://www.nbcnews.com/news/us-news/internet-now-officially-too-big-ip-addresses-run-out-n386081

10. **"Planted Up to the Very Door":** "How Arlington National Cemetery came to be" Smithsonian.com. November 2009. By Robert M. Poole. http://www.smithsonianmag.com/history/how-arlington-national-cemetery-came-to-be-145147007/?all

11. **Life After Luggage:** "Unclaimed Baggage Center" www.unclaimedbaggage.com/; "The 15 coolest things we found out about The Unclaimed Baggage Center." *Huffington Post.* July 21, 2014. By Carly Ledbetter. http://www.huffingtonpost.com/2014/07/21/unclaimed-baggage-center_n_5568695.html; "The nation's stash of lost luggage finds a new life in this Alabama town. Smithsonianmag.com. May 27, 2015. By Rachel Nuwer."

12. **The Missing Letter on Tests:** Mount Holyoke. https://www.mtholyoke.edu/; "College grade inflation: Does 'A' stand for 'average'?" *USA Today.* Nov. 21, 2013. By Cara Newton. "How come you never got an "E" in school?" *Mental Floss.* By Matt Soniak. http://mentalfloss.com/article/24960/how-come-you-never-got-e-school; "A to F scale gets poor marks but is likely to stay" *Washington Post.* Oct. 18, 2005. By Jay Mathews.

13. **Bargain Hunting at the NSA:** "National Cryptologic Museum" NSA.gov. https://www.nsa.gov/about/cryptologic-heritage/museum/; "'No Such Agency' spies on the communications of the world" *Washington Post.* June 6, 2013. By Anne Gearan; "The National Security Agency is established" Nov. 4, 1952. *Politico.* Nov. 4, 2010. By Andrew Glass. http://www.politico.com/story/2010/11/the-national-security-agency-is-established-nov-4-1952-044671; "The NSA will neither confirm nor deny these are items in its gift shop" *Business Insider.* May 25, 2016. By Paul Szoldra. http://www.businessinsider.com/nsa-gift-shop-2016-5

14. **The Day the South Invaded Vermont:** "The raid" The St. Albans Raid. http://www.stalbansraid.com/history/the-raid/

15. **Talking Trees:** "Mysteries of the trail-marker trees" *The Illinois Steward.* Summer 2006. By William McClain. http://web.extension.illinois.edu/illinoissteward/openarticle.cfm?ArticleID=26&Page=1; "Great Lakes Trail Marker Tree Society" http://www.greatlakestrailtreesociety.org/trail_tree_gallery.html; Interview Dennis Downes.

16. **31 Flavors, 365 Electors:** "Marker placed at Hyde Park shopping center where Obamas shared first kiss" *Chicago Tribune*. Aug. 16, 2012. By Dahleen Glanton; "What Barack and Michelle Obama think about Southside with You, the Sundance homage to their love story." *Vanity Fair*. Jan. 25, 2016. By Julie Miller.

17. **The Battle of Los Angeles:** "The Army Air Forces In World War II" Volume One. Eds. Wesley Frank Craven and James Lea Cate. Office of Air Force History. 1983. Pp. 282-286. https://web.archive.org/web/20090325191904/http://www.airforcehistory.hq.af.mil/Publications/fulltext/aaf_wwii-v1.pdf; Fort MacArthur Museum. http://www.ftmac.org/

18. **Of Friendship and Firebombs:** "Nobuo Fujita, 85, is dead; only foe to bomb America" *New York Times*. Oct. 3, 1997. By Nicholas D. Kristof.

19. **A Stroll to Siberia:** "Can you really see Russia from Alaska?" *Slate*. Sept. 15, 2008. By Nina Rastogi. http://www.slate.com/articles/news_and_politics/explainer/2008/09/can_you_really_see_russia_from_alaska.html; "Russian father-son team skis across the Bering Strait" *Juneau Empire*. March 26, 1998; "Karl Bushby is walking around the world. No, really." *Men's Journal*. By Grant Stoddard. http://www.mensjournal.com/expert-advice/karl-bushby-is-walking-around-the-world-no-really-20130514/celebrating-new-years-eve-in-montana-2003; "Karl Bushby questions his decision to walk around the world" *Outside*. May 15, 2015. By Jay Bennett. https://www.outsideonline.com/1981496/karl-bushby-questions-his-decision-walk-around-world

20. **Gem of the Mountain:** "Origins of the name 'Idaho' and how Idaho became a territory in 1863" Idaho Historical Society. By Merle W. Wells. http://imnh.isu.edu/digitalatlas/geog/explore/essay.pdf; "What does 'Idaho' really mean? Turns out, nothing" *The Oregonian*. March 27, 2010. By John Terry; "Oregon the name" The Oregon Encyclopedia. By Edwin Battistella. https://oregonencyclopedia.org/articles/oregon_the_name/#.WUEFd4zyuM9

21. **Eminent Distain:** "The story behind the Hess Triangle, once the littlest piece of land in NYC" Gothamist. April 9, 2015. By Jen Carlson. http://gothamist.com/2015/04/09/hess_triangle_history.php; "The Hess spite triangle, the smallest piece of New York City real estate" *The New Yorker*. Dec. 17, 2015. By Julia Wertz

22. **Maine Dunes:** Desert of Maine. http://www.desertofmaine.com/; "The science of a tourist trap: What's this desert doing in Maine?" *Smithsonian*. May 27, 2014. By Natasha Geiling. http://www.smithsonianmag.com/travel/why-desert-middle-maine-180951555/; "The little desert that grew in Maine" *New York Times*. Sept. 22, 2006. By Maura J. Casey

23. **The Secret behind Lincoln's Head:** "Mount Rushmore's secret room" (video). *Business Insider*. Jan. 31, 2017. http://www.businessinsider.com/secret-room-facts-mount-rushmore-presidents-south-dakota-inaccessible-tourists-lincoln-2017-1; "The hidden room behind Mount Rushmore. *Mental Floss*. By Jake Rossen. http://mentalfloss.com/article/91207/hidden-room-behind-mount-rushmore; "Mount Rushmore National Memorial" Visitrapidcity.com. https://www.visitrapidcity.com/mount-rushmore; "13 monumental facts about North by Northwest" Mental Floss. By Eric D. Snider. http://mentalfloss.com/article/77788/13-monumental-facts-about-north-northwest

24. **The Closet of Daryl Davis:** "'Every racist I know voted for Donald Trump'" *The Atlantic*. Feb. 13, 2017. By Conor Friedersdorf; "A black man's quixotic quest to quell the racism of the KKK, one robe at a time" *Los Angeles Times*. Dec. 8, 2016. By Jeffrey Fleishman; "KKK member walks up to black musician in a bar – but it's not a joke, and what happens next will astound you" *Liberty Voice*. Nov. 20, 2013. By Rebecca Savastio. http://guardianlv.com/2013/11/kkk-member-walks-up-to-black-musician-in-bar-but-its-not-a-joke-and-what-happens-next-will-astound-you/

25. **The Many Facets of Fasces:** "Why the Lincoln Memorial was almost never built" Vox.com. Oct. 3, 2016. By Phil Edwards. http://www.vox.com/2016/10/3/13124866/lincoln-memorial-joe-cannon; "History of the Swastika" United States Holocaust Memorial Museum. https://www.ushmm.org/wlc/en/article.php?ModuleId=10007453; "When fasces aren't fascist" *City Journal*. Spring 2014. By Eugene Kontorovich. https://www.city-journal.org/html/when-fasces-aren%E2%80%99t-fascist-13651.html; "Secret symbol of the Lincoln Memorial" National Park Service. July 23, 2013. By Nathan King. https://www.nps.gov/nama/blogs/secret-symbol-of-the-lincoln-memorial.htm

26. **A Night at the Museum:** "City Museum." http://www.citymuseum.org; "St. Louis' Wondrous City Museum." *Chicago*. Oct. 2, 2012. By Whet Moser. http://www.chicagomag.com/Chicago-Magazine/The-312/October-2012/St-Louis-Wonderous-City-Museum/; "11 awesomely unexpected things in St. Louis's City Museum." *Mental Floss*. By Erin McCarthy. http://mentalfloss.com/article/13063/11-awesomely-unexpected-things-st-louis%E2%80%99s-city-museum

27. **When Connecticut Owned Ohio:** "Boundaries of Georgia." New Georgia Encyclopedia. Sept. 27, 2013. By William J. Morton. Edited by Chris Dobbs. http://www.georgiaencyclopedia.org/articles/history-archaeology/boundaries-georgia; "Our history" Case Western Reserve University. http://case.edu/about/history.html; "Western lands" Dictionary of American History. Jun 13, 2017. Encyclopedia.com. http://www.encyclopedia.com/history/dictionaries-thesauruses-pictures-and-press-releases/western-lands; "Connecticut" By Albert E. Van Dusen. (New York: Random House, 1961) via CT State Library. http://libguides.ctstatelibrary.org/hg/maps/westernlands; "New Connecticut on Lake Erie: Connecticut's Western Reserve" Connecticut History. By Barbara Austen. https://connecticuthistory.org/new-connecticut-on-lake-erie-connecticuts-western-reserve/; "What is the Western Reserve?" Western Reserve Historical Society. https://www.wrhs.org/about/wrhs-history/; "What is the Western Reserve?" Trip Savvy. June 8, 2017. By Sandy Mitchell. https://www.tripsavvy.com/what-is-the-western-reserve-752620

28. **Iowa–The Final Frontier:** "Welcome to Trekfest XXXIII" http://trekfest.org/; "James T. Kirk's Hometown (in 200 years)" *Chicago Tribune*. July 8, 2004. By Raoul Mowatt; "Star Trek history: Take a road trip to Riverside, Iowa" *Denver Post*. Sept. 1, 2013. By Laura Keeney. http://blogs.denverpost.com/nerd/2013/09/01/star-trek-history-take-a-roadtrip-to-riverside-iowa/949/

29. **Pyramids and Politics:** "Stanley R. Mickelsen Safeguard Complex: A strange pyramid built in the middle of nowhere" Weather.com. April 21, 2014. https://weather.com/news/news/stanley-r-mickelsen-safeguard-complex-pyramid-build-middle-no-where-20140420; "A pyramid in the middle of nowhere built to track the end of the world. *Gizmodo*. Apr. 13, 2014. By Geoff Manaugh. http://gizmodo.com/a-pyramid-in-the-middle-of-nowhere-built-to-track-the-e-1562753133; Mickelsen Unofficial Site. http://srmsc.org; "The pyramid at the end of the world" *Fusion*. Oct. 30, 2016. By Elmo Keep. http://fusion.net/interactive/361728/north-dakota-pyramid-on-the-prairie/

30. **The Man with No Brand:** "Who you callin' a maverick?" *The New York Times*. Oct. 4, 2008. By John Schwartz; "Original 'Maverick' was unconventional Texan." NPR. Sept. 5, 2008. http://www.npr.org/templates/story/story.php?storyId=94312345; "Maverick, Samuel Augustus," Texas State Historical Association. By Paula Mitchell Marks. https://tshaonline.org/handbook/online/articles/fma84

31. **Oaken Ownership:** "The tree that owns itself" Athens Convention and Visitors Bureau. https://www.visitathensga.com/listings/the-tree-that-owns-itself/234/; "The tree that owns itself" *Mental Floss*. By Kate Horowitz. http://mentalfloss.com/article/68698/tree-owns-itself

32. **Sleeping with the Fishes:** "Jules Undersea Lodge" http://www.jul.com; "Underwater world record broken in Florida Keys" CBS News. Dec. 15, 2014. By David Sutta. http://miami.cbslocal.com/2014/12/15/underwater-world-record-to-be-broken-in-florida-keys/; "Jules Undersea Lodge is a one-of-a-kind recreational hotel for divers" The Florida Keys & Key West. Jan. 3, 2017. http://www.fla-keys.com/news/article/9420/

33. **Free Parking in New Jersey:** "$500 for rolling double ones and $400 for landing on Go: The new Monopoly 'house rules' made up by fans of the Hasbro game" Associated Press via the *Daily Mail*. Apr. 4, 2014. http://www.dailymail.co.uk/femail/article-2596909/Hasbro-picks-5-house-rules-new-Monopoly-set.html; "Ever cheat at Monopoly? So did its creator: He stole the idea from a woman" NPR. Mar. 3, 2015. http://www.npr.org/2015/03/03/382662772/ever-cheat-at-monopoly-so-did-its-creator-he-stole-the-idea-from-a-woman; "Monopoly and Atlantic City, 75 tough years later" AOL. Feb. 23, 2010. By Bruce Watson. https://www.aol.com/article/2010/02/23/atlantic-city-and-monopoly-a-zero-sum-game-on-the-jersey-shore/19309242/; "Can you tour Atlantic City using a Monopoly board?" Associated Press via NBC News. Oct. 6, 2010. http://www.nbcnews.com/id/39539576/ns/travel-destination_travel/t/can-you-tour-atlantic-city-using-monopoly-board/#.WMwol_nyuM9; "80 years later, how would Atlantic City-based Monopoly look?" Associated Press via *The Arizona Republic*. Mar. 23, 2015. By Wayne Parry

34. **Biking the Apocalypse:** "Tunnel Vision" PennLive. Apr. 10, 2015. By Nick Malawskey. http://www.pennlive.com/projects/2015/pa-turnpike-tunnels/; "Back in time" Federal Highway Administration. By Rickie Longfellow. https://www.fhwa.dot.gov/infrastructure/back1007.cfm; "Pike2Bike" http://www.pike2bike.com/home.html; "Visiting the abandoned turnpike near Breezewood, Pennsylvania." Uncovering PA. Apr. 6. By Jim Cheney. http://uncoveringpa.com/abandoned-pa-turnpike; "The Pennsylvania Turnpike" *Washington Post*. Aug. 17, 2005. By Christine H. O'Toole

35. **The Immortal Woman:** "Henrietta Lacks' 'immortal' cells. *Smithsonian*. Jan. 22, 2010. By Sarah Zielinski. http://www.smithsonianmag.com/science-nature/henrietta-lacks-immortal-cells-6421299/; "Henrietta Lacks' family finally gets say in genetic destiny. Can we control our own?" CNN. Aug. 11, 2013. By Stephanie Smith. http://www.cnn.com/2013/08/07/health/henrietta-lacks-genetic-destiny/; "'Henrietta Lacks': A donor's immortal legacy" NPR. Feb. 2, 2010. Excerpted from "The Immortal Life of Henrietta Lacks by Rebecca Skloot. Copyright 2010. Crown, a division of Random House. http://www.npr.org/2010/02/02/123232331/henrietta-lacks-a-donors-immortal-legacy

36. **Icon of Invention:** "This Day in Jewish History//2000: Hedy Lamarr, actress and inventor of torpedo anti-jamming technology, dies" *Haaretz*. Jan. 19, 2014. By David B. Green; "Remembering Hedy Lamarr: Actress, weapons systems developer" NPR. Nov. 9, 2014. http://www.npr.org/2014/11/09/362828941/remembering-hedy-lamarr-actress-weapons-systems-developer; "National Inventors Hall of Fame announces 2014 inductees" The National Inventors Hall of Fame via PR Newswire. Mar. 4, 2014. http://www.prnewswire.com/news-releases/national-inventors-hall-of-fame-announces-2014-inductees-248359561.html; "Most beautiful woman by day, inventor by night" NPR. Nov. 22, 2011. http://www.npr.org/2011/11/27/142664182/most-beautiful-woman-by-day-inventor-by-night; "Hedy Lamarr: movie star, inventor of WiFi" CBS News. Apr. 20, 2012. http://www.cbsnews.com/news/hedy-lamarr-movie-star-inventor-of-wifi/2/

37. **All Quiet on the West Virginia Front:** "Enter the quiet zone: Where cell service, Wi-Fi are banned" NPR. Oct. 8, 2013. By Elise Hu. http://www.npr.org/sections/alltechconsidered/2013/10/08/218976699/enter-the-quiet-zone-where-cell-service-wi-fi-are-banned; "Life in the quiet zone: West Virginia town avoids electronics for science" *National Geographic*. Oct. 11, 2014. By Sasha Ingber; "'Electrosensitives' flock to Wi-Fi quiet zone as teens set up rogue hotspots" *Ars Technica*. Jan. 5, 2015. Jon Brodkin. https://arstechnica.com/information-technology/2015/01/electrosensitives-seek-haven-in-wi-fi-quiet-zone-as-teens-set-up-hotspots/; "There's Wi-Fi in the middle of the only place in the U.S. where Wi-Fi is 'outlawed'" *Fusion*. Dec. 22, 2015. By Kashmir Hill. http://fusion.net/story/243321/wtf-wifi-in-the-green-bank-wv-quiet-zone/; "The quiet zone" *Wired*. Feb. 1, 2004. By John Geirland. https://www.wired.com/2004/02/quiet/

38. **The Great Molasses Flood:** "Boston's Great Molasses Flood of 1919" *Mental Floss*. By Ethan Trex. http://mentalfloss.com/article/27366/bostons-great-molasses-flood-1919; "Solving a mystery behind the deadly 'tsunami of molasses' of 1919" *New York Times*. Nov. 26, 2016. By Erin McCann; "It's been exactly 98 years since a giant wave of molasses killed 21 people in Boston" Boston.com. Jan. 15, 2017. By Nik DeCosta-Klipa. https://www.boston.com/news/history/2017/01/15/its-been-exactly-98-years-since-a-giant-wave-of-molasses-killed-21-people-in-boston

39. **A Divided Banner:** "Maryland's flag has a subtle symbol of Confederate sympathy" *Washingtonian*. Aug. 19, 2015. By Andrew Beaujon. https://www.washingtonian.com/2015/08/19/marylands-flag-confederate-symbol-crossland-banner-calvert-family/; "A symbol of rebels is on most Md. tags Cross indicated Confederate leanings during Civil War" *Baltimore Sun*. Jan. 4, 1997. By Jon Morgan; "The Lincoln Administration and arbitrary arrests: A reconsideration" Journal of the Abraham Lincoln Association. 1983. By Mark E. Neely, Jr. https://quod.lib.umich.edu/j/jala/2629860.0005.103/--lincoln-administration-and-arbitrary-arrests?rgn=main;view=fulltext

40. **Chopped Chicken:** "Mike the Headless Chicken" http://www.miketheheadlesschicken.org/; "Chicken more popular than beef in U.S. for first time in 100 years" *Huffington Post*. Jan. 2, 2014. By Alison Spiegel. http://www.huffingtonpost.com/2014/01/02/chicken-vs-beef_n_4525366.html

41. **Butter Battles:** "The butter wars: When margarine was pink" *National Geographic*. Aug. 13, 2014. By Rebecca Rupp; "The surprisingly interesting history of margarine" *Mental Floss*. By Ethan Trex. http://mentalfloss.com/article/25638/surprisingly-interesting-history-margarine; "Legislators seek to end state's butter-only law for restaurants, prisons" *Milwaukee Journal Sentinel*. Sept. 19, 2011. By Karen Herzog; "What's the story with no butter in schools, jails?" *Fond du Lac Reporter*. Feb. 8, 2015. By Colleen Kottke; "State ban on oleo margarine led to smuggling" *Wisconsin Life*. June 24, 2015. http://www.wisconsinlife.org/story/state-ban-oleo-margarine-led-smuggling/; "Wisconsin's Irish butter lawsuit: Kerrygold is banned under unique state law" Associated Press via TwinCities.com. Mar. 17, 2017. http://www.twincities.com/2017/03/17/wisconsin-irish-butter-ban-lawsuit/

42. **Highway to the Danger Zone:** "Loophole may allow US crime spree" BBC News. May 9, 2005. By Matthew Davis. http://news.bbc.co.uk/2/hi/americas/4529829.stm; "Is Yellowstone ripe for a crime spree?" NPR. May 10, 2005. By Robert Siegel. http://www.npr.org/templates/story/story.php?storyId=4647041; "The best place to commit a crime in America? Yellowstone National Park" *Conde Nast Traveler* via Fox News. Nov. 22, 2016. By Ken Jennings. http://www.foxnews.com/travel/2016/11/22/best-place-to-commit-crime-in-america-yellowstone-national-park.html

43. **Online Origins:** "This is the room where the Internet was born" *Gizmodo.* Mar. 5, 2014. By Alissa Walker. http://gizmodo.com/this-is-the-room-where-the-internet-was-born-1527205592

44. **The West Wings:** "Alaska Chilkat Bald Eagle Preserve" Alaska Department of Natural Resources. http://dnr.alaska.gov/parks/units/eagleprv.htm; "Bald eagle: A mighty symbol, with a not-so-mighty voice" NPR. July 2, 2012. By Jessica Robinson. http://www.npr.org/templates/story/story.php?storyId=156187375; "American myths: Benjamin Franklin's turkey and the presidential seal" *Smithsonian.* Jan. 25, 2013. By Jimmy Stamp. http://www.smithsonianmag.com/arts-culture/american-myths-benjamin-franklins-turkey-and-the-presidential-seal-6623414/

45. **Small-Town Life:** "America's tiniest town is sold and renamed PhinDeli Town Buford, Wyoming" *Daily Beast.* Oct. 17, 2013. By Nina Strochlic. http://www.thedailybeast.com/articles/2013/10/17/america-s-tiniest-town-is-sold-and-renamed-phindeli-town-buford-wyoming.html; "Monowi, Neb.: Population 1" CBS News. Oct. 29, 2006. By Caitlin Johnson. http://www.cbsnews.com/news/monowi-neb-population-1/; "Monowi Boyd County" University of Nebraska-Lincoln. By Jane Graff. http://www.casde.unl.edu/history/counties/boyd/monowi/; "Monowi: The village of one" Nebraskaland. Nov. 18, 2014. By Amy Kucera. http://magazine.outdoornebraska.gov/2014/11/monowi-village-one/

46. **Hog Wild:** "The Pig War" National Park Service. Nov. 4, 2016. https://www.nps.gov/sajh/learn/historyculture/the-pig-war.htm

47. **Of Paramount Importance:** "Paramount's logo has given millions a peek at Ogden peak" *Deseret News.* Sept. 8, 2008. By Lynn Arave; "Utah sets state record for tourist visits in 2012" *Deseret News.* Sept. 17, 2013. By Jasen Lee; "Paramount Pictures announces new logo" *Entertainment Weekly.* Dec. 14, 2011. By Adam B. Vary. http://ew.com/article/2011/12/14/paramount-studios-new-logo/; "Mountain to moon: 10 movie studio logos and the stories behind them" *TIME Magazine.* Sept. 21, 2012. By Wook Kim; "Ben Lomond Peak" Utah.com. https://utah.com/hiking/ben-lomond-peak; "Engulfed: The Death of Paramount Pictures and the Birth of Corporate Hollywood" by Bernard F. Dick. The University Press of Kentucky. Copyright 2001. P. 9.

48. **The Nation's Busiest Empty Place:** "The story behind the strangely empty Times Square Building where the New Year's Eve Ball drops every year" *Business Insider.* Dec. 29, 2014. By Paige Cooperstein. http://www.businessinsider.com/new-years-eve-ball-at-one-times-square-2014-12; "Inside the home of the New Year's Eve Ball" *The New Yorker.* Dec. 20, 2013. By Nate Lavey; "Here's how much it actually costs to buy one of those Times Square billboards" *Business Insider.* Dec. 31, 2012. By Jim Edwards. http://www.businessinsider.com/what-it-costs-to-advertise-in-times-square-2012-12; "The surprising origins of the New Year's Eve Ball drop tradition" *TIME Magazine.* Dec. 30, 2016. By Olivia B. Waxman

49. **The Burning Town:** "Fire in the hole" *Smithsonian.* May 2005. By Kevin Krajick. http://www.smithsonianmag.com/science-nature/fire-in-the-hole-77895126/; "Centralia loses another resident, home abandoned" Centraliapa.org. Jan. 2, 2017. By Centralia Pa. http://www.centraliapa.org/centralia-loses-another-resident-home-abandoned/; "Graffiti Highway, Centralia Pennsylvania." Centraliapa.org. Oct. 25, 2014. By Centralia Pa. http://www.centraliapa.org/graffiti-highway-centralia-pennsylvania/

50. **Deli Meats in Space:** "That time an astronaut smuggled a corned beef sandwich in space" *Smithsonian.* March 25, 2015. By Marissa Fessenden. http://www.smithsonianmag.com/smart-news/time-when-astronaut-smuggled-corned-beef-sandwich-space-180954749/; "A contraband corned beef sandwich went to space 50 years ago" *Popular Mechanics.* Mar. 24, 2015. By John Wenz; "Space food: From squeeze tubes to celebrity chefs" Nov. 23, 2006. By Robert Z. Pearlman. http://www.space.com/3150-space-food-squeeze-tubes-celebrity-chefs.html

51. **The Bad Boy of Krypton:** "$412 check that bought Superman sold for $160,000" Associated Press via *San Diego Union-Tribune.* Apr. 17, 2012; "Superman" Jewish Virtual Library. By Blair Kramer. http://www.jewishvirtuallibrary.org/superman; "Superman's birthday puts spotlight on creators' roots" Associated Press via *New York Daily News.* Apr. 17, 2013; "July 9, 2003: Ohio historical Superman marker" Superman Hompage. https://www.supermanhomepage.com/news/2003-news/2003-news-merchandise.php?topic=2003-news-merchandise/0709

52. **A Little Green:** "Experience Forest Park" Forest Park Conservancy. http://www.forestparkconservancy.org/forest-park/; "Mill Ends Park" The Oregon Encyclopedia. By Eric A. Kimmel. https://oregonencyclopedia.org/articles/mill_ends_park/#.WNgWZvnyuM8; "One person arrested after Occupy Portland flash mob in Mill Ends Park" *The Oregonian.* Dec. 16, 2011. By Kate Mather; "Tree stolen from Mill Ends Park replaced – for the good of leprechauns, officials say" *The Oregonian.* Mar. 7, 2013. By Sara Hottman; "Mill Ends Park" City of Portland. https://www.portlandoregon.gov/parks/finder/index.cfm?&propertyid=265&action=ViewPark; "One step and you've left Mill Ends Park. Associated Press via *Los Angeles Times.* May 6, 2001. By Amalie Young

53. **A Misnamed Malady:** "Frank Buckles, last World War I doughboy, is dead at 110" *New York Times.* Feb. 28, 2011. By Richard Goldstein; "Origins of the 1918 pandemic: The case for France" NPR. Feb. 20, 2006. By Vikki Valentine. http://www.npr.org/templates/story/story.php?storyId=5222069; "Why was it called the 'Spanish Flu'?" History.com. Jan. 15, 2016. By Evan Andrews. http://www.history.com/news/ask-history/why-was-it-called-the-spanish-flu; "The site of origin of the 1918 influenza pandemic and its public health implications" Journal of Translational Medicine via National Institutes of Health. Jan. 20, 2004. By John M. Barry. https://www.ncbi.nlm.nih.gov/pmc/articles/PMC340389/#

54. **The Unseen Wall:** "There's a hidden wire stretched above American cities – and few people know what it's for" *Business Insider.* Oct. 16, 2015. By Jenner Deal. http://www.businessinsider.com/jewish-eruv-wire-hidden-in-manhattan-religious-carrying-sabbath-2015-10; "What is an eruv?" My Jewish Learning. By Sharonne Cohen. http://www.myjewishlearning.com/article/eruv/; "High wire strewn through city lets Jews keep the faith" *New York Post.* May 24, 2015. By Isabel Vincent and Melissa Klein.

55. **The Fast and the Felonious:** "A timeline of NASCAR" NASCAR.com. Jan. 5, 2015. http://www.nascar.com/en_us/monster-energy-nascar-cup-series/nascar-nation/nascar-edu/nascar-basic/how-nascar-was-started.html; "NASCAR's earliest days forever connected to bootlegging" NASCAR.com. Nov. 1, 2012. By Rick Houston. http://www.nascar.com/en_us/news-media/articles/2012/11/01/moonshine-mystique.html; "How NASCAR landed a staggering TV deal despite ratings decline" *Sporting News.* Aug. 15, 2013. By Bob Pockrass. http://www.sportingnews.com/nascar/news/4517344-nascar-tv-coverage-network-contract-fox-sports-1-nbc-deal-ratings; "For Junior, a presidential pardon was a great start to the 1986 season" Motor Sports Unplugged. Apr. 19, 2012. By Junior Johnson. http://motorsportsunplugged.com/tag/president-reagan-junior-johnson/

56. **The Morning of Two Sunrises:** "Trinity Site open house" White Sands Missile Range. http://www.wsmr.army.mil/PAO/Trinity/Pages/Home.aspx; "The Trinity Test" History.com. http://www.history.com/topics/world-war-ii/trinity-test; "Today's nukes are thousands of times more powerful than WWII A-bombs" *Popular Mechanics.* Oct. 10, 2016. By Jay Bennett

57. **"Nobody Shot Me":** "The St. Valentine's Day Massacre" History.com. http://www.history.com/this-day-in-history/the-st-valentines-day-massacre; "The Mob Museum" http://themobmuseum.org/; "Gangland Chicago: Criminality and Lawlessness in the

Windy City" By Richard C. Lindberg. p. 336. Lanham, Md.: Rowman & Littlefield. Copyright 2016; "St. Valentine's Massacre bricks may not attract a load of interest" *Chicago Tribune*. Feb. 21, 1996. By John O'Brien

58. **The Richest Hill on Earth:** Pitwatch. www.Pitwatch.org; "Thousands of Montana snow geese die after landing in toxic, acidic mine pit" *Washington Post*. Dec. 7, 2016. By Ben Guarino; "The goose-killing lake and the scientists who study it" *The Atlantic*. Dec. 13, 2016. By Sarah Zhang

59. **"Continue, Please":** "Milgram experiment 50 years on" *Yale Daily News*. Sept. 28, 2011. By Ben Prawdzik. http://yaledailynews.com/blog/2011/09/28/milgram-experiment-50-years-on/; McLeod, S. A. (2007). The Milgram Experiment. Retrieved from www.simplypsychology.org/milgram.html; "The shocking truth of the notorious Milgram Obedience Experiments. *Discover Magazine*. Oct. 2, 2013. By Gina Perry. http://blogs.discovermagazine.com/crux/2013/10/02/the-shocking-truth-of-the-notorious-milgram-obedience-experiments/#.WOnlZ9IrKM9l; "Was Milgram's research ethical?" 2007. Intropsych.com. http://www.intropsych.com/ch15_social/research_ethics.html; "Six degrees: Urban myth?" *Psychology Today*. Mar. 1, 2002. By Judith Kleinfeld. https://www.psychologytoday.com/articles/200203/six-degrees-urban-myth

60. **Man of the People:** "From the vault: Jerry Springer, Cincinnati city council member, caught paying checks for sex in 1974" WCPO Cincinnati. Apr. 28, 2016. By Greg Noble. http://www.wcpo.com/lifestyle/from-the-vault/from-the-vault-jerry-springer-cincinnati-city-council-member-caught-paying-checks-for-sex-in-1974; "Jerry Springer" Biography.com. A&E Television Network. Apr. 2, 2014. http://www.biography.com/people/jerry-springer-498154; "Jerry Springer: Celebrating 20 years of 'trash TV'" CNN. Nov. 3, 2010. By Lisa Respers France. http://www.cnn.com/2010/SHOWBIZ/TV/11/02/jerry.springer.anniversary/; "Jerry Springer: 'This might seem strange'" *Cincinnati Enquirer*. Dec. 25, 2015. By Polly Campbell

61. **Frozen Dead Guy Days:** "Frozen Dead Guy Days" http://frozendeadguydays.org/; "Vital signs strong at Nederland's Frozen Dead Guy Days" *Daily Camera*. Mar. 11, 2017. By Amanda Trejos. http://www.dailycamera.com/boulder-county-news/ci_30850769/vital-signs-strong-at-nederlands-frozen-dead-guy; "Oddball events animate Frozen Dead Guy Days in Nederland" *Daily Camera*. Mar. 9, 2017. By Christy Fantz. http://www.dailycamera.com/entertainment/ci_30844522/

62. **Personification of a Nation:** "United States nicknamed Uncle Sam" History.com. http://www.history.com/this-day-in-history/united-states-nicknamed-uncle-sam; "The City of Troy, New York – Home of Uncle Sam" Library of Congress. By Michael R. McNulty. http://memory.loc.gov/diglib/legacies/loc.afc.afc-legacies.200003395/; "US election: Why a Republican elephant and Democratic donkey?" BBC. Nov. 3, 2016. http://www.bbc.co.uk/newsround/37848449; "Uncle Sam birthplace statue – Arlington, MA" Waymarking.com. By neoc1.

63. **No Holier Place:** "Robert Gould Shaw" Civil War Trust. http://www.civilwar.org/education/history/biographies/robert-gould-shaw.html?referrer=https://www.google.com/; "Fort Wagner and the 54th Massachusetts Volunteer Infantry" Civil War Trust. By Brian C. Pohanka. http://www.civilwar.org/battlefields/batterywagner/battery-wagner-history-articles/fortwagnerpohanka.html?referrer=http://www.civilwar.org/battlefields/battery-wagner.html; "The 54th Massachusetts Infantry" History.com. http://www.history.com/topics/american-civil-war/the-54th-massachusetts-infantry; "For black Civil War soldiers, respect was the first victory" *Washington Post*. Sept. 13, 2013. By Sally Jenkins; "Meet Sgt. William Carney: The first African-American Medal of Honor recipient" Department of Defense. Feb. 8, 2017. By Katie Lang. https://www.defense.gov/News/Article/Article/1075726/meet-sgt-william-carney-the-first-african-american-medal-of-honor-recipient; "Robert Gould Shaw and the 54th Regiment" National Park Service. https://www.nps.gov/boaf/learn/historyculture/shaw.htm; "'If slaves will make good soldiers our whole theory of slavery is wrong'" Civil War Daily Gazette. http://civilwardailygazette.com/if-slaves-will-make-good-soldiers-our-whole-theory-of-slavery-is-wrong/

64. **Numbers on the Air:** "The spooky world of the 'numbers stations'" BBC News Magazine. Apr. 16, 2014. By Olivia Sorrel-Dejerine. http://www.bbc.com/news/magazine-24910397; "Atencion: seis siete tres siete cero: The shortwave numbers mystery. NPR. By David Goren. http://www.npr.org/programs/lnfsound/stories/000526.stories.html; "The stupidly simple spy messages no computer could decode" *The Daily Beast*. Mar. 6, 2016. By Shane Harris. http://www.thedailybeast.com/articles/2016/03/06/the-stupidly-simple-spy-messages-no-computer-could-decode.html

65. **The Ultimate Treehouse:** "Welcome to Humboldt County & the Famous One Log House" http://www.oneloghouse.com/; "Frequently asked questions" National Park Service. https://www.nps.gov/redw/faqs.htm

66. **A Tilting Point in History:** "Why I spared the Leaning Tower of Pisa" *The Guardian*. Jan. 12, 2000. By Rory Carroll. https://www.theguardian.com/theguardian/2000/jan/13/features11.g23; "13 straight facts about the Leaning Tower of Pisa" *Mental Floss*. By Michael Arbeiter. http://mentalfloss.com/article/70395/13-straight-facts-about-leaning-tower-pisa; "Author Leon Weckstein" http://www.leonweckstein.com/; "Village intends to buy Leaning Tower of Niles, spend $550K in repairs" *Chicago Tribune/Niles Herald Spectator*. By Lee V. Gaines.

67. **Sock It to Me:** "History" U.S. Soccer. https://www.ussoccer.com/about/history/timeline; "First smackdown 1869" *Princeton Magazine*. By Wendy Plump. http://www.princetonmagazine.com/first-smackdown-1869/; "Why Americans call soccer 'soccer'" *The Atlantic*. Jun. 13, 2014. By Uri Friedman; "First intercollegiate football game" Princeton.edu. http://www.princeton.edu/~oktour/virtualtour/korean/Hist14-Football.htm; "What would the father of American football make of the modern game? *The New Yorker*. Nov. 19, 2015. By Ian Crouch; "A brief history of the game" Hornetfootball.org. http://www.hornetfootball.org/documents/football-history.htm

68. **The Most Famous Marquee:** "Thomas Edison drove the film industry to California" *Mental Floss*. By Dan Lewis. http://mentalfloss.com/article/51722/thomas-edison-drove-film-industry-california; "The Hollywood sign originally read "HOLLY-WOODLAND" *Gizmodo*. Jun. 4, 2014. By Nathan Masters. http://gizmodo.com/the-hollywood-sign-originally-read-hollywood-land-1585421650; "Will actress who killed herself on Hollywood sign finally get her name lights? Snubbed thirties starlet who threw herself from iconic sign to be subject of new blockbuster" *Daily Mail*. Sept. 20, 2014. By Mia de Graaf. http://www.dailymail.co.uk/news/article-2763443/Struggling-actress-jumped-death-Hollywood-sign-82-years-ago-finally-lands-starring-role-industry-heavyweights-sign-turn-life-movie.html

69. **A Visitor from the Sky People:** "Willamette Meteorite Agreement" American Museum of Natural History. Jun. 22, 2000. http://www.amnh.org/exhibitions/permanent-exhibitions/rose-center-for-earth-and-space/dorothy-and-lewis-b.-cullman-hall-of-the-universe/willamette-meteorite-agreement/; "The Willamette Meteorite" American Museum of Natural History. http://www.amnh.org/exhibitions/permanent-exhibitions/rose-center-for-earth-and-space/dorothy-and-lewis-b.-cullman-hall-of-the-universe/planets/planetary-impacts/the-willamette-meteorite; "It came from the sky!" *The Daily Beast*. Feb. 17, 2013. By Michael Daly. http://www.thedailybeast.com/articles/2013/02/17/it-came-from-the-sky-the-meteorite-that-mangled-the-malibu-vertical-dek-

when-marie-kanpp-s-teenage-daughter-told-her-i-think-a-meteorite-hit-my-car-she-was-telling-the-truth-michael-daly-reports. html; "Meteorite crashes into Chevy Malibu" History.com. http://www.history.com/this-day-in-history/meteorite-crashes-into-chevy-malibu

70. **Rock 'n' Toll:** "The true story of history's only known meteorite victim." *National Geographic.* Feb. 20, 2013. By Justin Nobel; "Alabama Museum of Natural History" https://almnh.ua.edu/; "62 years ago today, Ann Hodges was hit by a meteorite" *Mental Floss.* By Kate Horowitz. http://mentalfloss.com/article/89383/62-years-ago-today-ann-hodges-was-hit-meteorite; "What are the odds a meteorite could kill you?" *National Geographic.* Feb. 9, 2016. By Brian Clark Howard

71. **Meeting at the Tripoint:** "The Tri-State Trail" Friends of White Clay Creek Preserve. http://friendsofpawccp-org.doodlekit.com/home/the-tristate-trail; "New trail provides first public access to Mason-Dixon Tri-State Marker" *Newark Post.* Jun. 9, 2015. By Josh Shannon. http://www.newarkpostonline.com/news/article_a5ec3a04-fe1a-58d4-a317-93ce887c863.html; "Maryland's waist: Narrow strip is geographic anomaly. *Los Angeles Times.* Oct. 8, 1987. By Charles Hillinger; "The Birth of 'Dixie'" *New York Times.* Mar. 31, 2012. By Christian McWhirter. https://opinionator.blogs.nytimes.com/2012/03/31/the-birth-of-dixie/?_r=0; "A brief history of the Mason-Dixie Line" University of Delaware. By John Mackenzie. http://www1.udel.edu/johnmack/mason_dixon/

72. **Rage with Relish:** "The Wiener's Circle, Chicago's rudest hot dog stand, is sold" *Chicago Tribune,* Sept. 18, 2015. By Kevin Pang; "The Wiener's Circle" http://www.thewienerscirclechicago.com/; "The Wiener's Circle welcomes Donald Trump with 3-inch Chicago hot dog" *Time Out.* Mar. 10, 2016. By Nick Kotecki. https://www.timeout.com/chicago/blog/the-wieners-circle-welcomes-donald-trump-with-3-inch-chicago-hot-dog-031016; "The most depressing hot dog stand in America" *Salon.* Sept. 29, 2010. By Francis Lam. http://www.salon.com/2010/09/29/chicago_hot_dog_wieners_circle/

73. **Crossing the Line:** "Haskell Free Library & Opera House" http://haskellopera.com/; "The U.S.-Canada border runs directly through this library" *Mental Floss.* By Taylor Berman. http://mentalfloss.com/article/76889/us-canada-border-runs-directly-through-library; "Woman charged with gun smuggling in Derby Line" *The Newport Daily Express.* http://newportvermontdailyexpress.com/content/woman-charged-gun-smuggling-derby-line; "Border towns struggle with post-9/11 security measures" *Toronto Star.* Sept. 2, 2011. By Andrew Chung; "'Don't touch Me,' said Canada. 'I won't!' said the U.S.A. so they moved 20 feet apart" NPR. Apr. 25, 2014. By Robert Krulwich. http://www.npr.org/sections/krulwich/2014/04/25/306535819/-don-t-touch-me-said-canada-i-won-t-said-the-usa-so-they-moved-20-feet-apart

74. **A Letter of Intent:** "Just how many bridges are there in Pittsburgh?" WTAE News. Sep. 13, 2006. http://www.wtae.com/article/just-how-many-bridges-are-there-in-pittsburgh/7424896; "Can you correctly spell the new top 10 most misspelled American cities list?" King Digital Entertainment via PR Newswire. Jun. 24, 2015. http://www.prnewswire.com/news-releases/can-you-correctly-spell-the-new-top-10-most-misspelled-american-cities-list-300103924.html; "How Pittsburgh got its "H" back" *Mental Floss.* By Stacy Conradt. http://mentalfloss.com/article/52943/how-pittsburgh-got-its-h-back-and-7-other-geographic-naming-oddities; "The controversial spelling of 'Pittsburgh', or why the 'H'?" Pittsburgh History & Landmarks Foundation. Dec. 21, 2000. By James Van Trump. http://phlf.org/2000/12/21/the-controversial-spelling-of-pittsburgh-or-why-the-h/

75. **Hamburger Helper:** "White Castle" www.whitecastle.com; "The origins of cult-favorite fast food restaurants: White Castle" Minyanville. Nov. 23, 2010. By Ryan Goldberg. http://www.minyanville.com/special-features/articles/white-castle-mcdonalds-fast-food-harold/11/23/2010/id/31227?refresh=1; "White Castle marks 90th anniversary with one-day return to Wichita" *Wichita Eagle.* May 12, 2011. By Beccy Tanner; "The White Castle story: the birth of fast food & the burger revolution" *Consumerist.* July 14, 2015. By Ashlee Kieler. https://consumerist.com/2015/07/14/the-white-castle-story-the-birth-of-fast-food-the-burger-revolution/

76. **The Amazon Queen of California:** "How all 50 states got their names" *Mental Floss.* By Matt Soniak. http://mentalfloss.com/article/31100/how-all-50-states-got-their-names; "California, Calafia, Khalif: The origin of the name 'California" KCET. Dec. 15, 2015. By Robert Petersen. https://www.kcet.org/shows/departures/california-calafia-khalif-the-origin-of-the-name-california; "California: The Name" by Ruth Putnam and Herbert I. Priestley. 1917. University of California Press Berkeley.

77. **Staying Sticky:** "Market lost & found" *Seattle Times.* Aug. 6, 2007. By Stuart Eskenazi; "Kissing, chewing – the 'germiest' tourist attractions" CNN. July 20, 2009. By Stephanie Chen. http://edition.cnn.com/2009/TRAVEL/07/20/germy.tourist.spots/; "There's already more gum on Seattle's newly-cleaned gum wall" *TIME Magazine.* Nov. 17, 2015. By Samantha Grossman; "Seattle gum-wall time-lapse: Watch ton of gum disappear in a minute" *Seattle Times.* Nov. 16, 2015. By Evan Bush

78. **Harvey's Hard Day:** "Remembering the night Harvey Haddix threw 12 perfect innings for the Pirates … and lost" MLB.com. May 26, 2015. By Chris Landers. http://m.mlb.com/cutfour/2015/05/26/126504134/harvey-haddix-threw-12-perfect-innings-and-lost; "In 1959 Harvey Haddix pitched perhaps the best game ever – and lost" *Pittsburgh Post-Gazette.* May 24, 2009. By Bob Dvorchak; "Brewers unveil plaque to memorialize the final home run of Hank Aaron's career, #755" Milwaukee Brewers. Jun. 7, 2007. http://milwaukee.brewers.mlb.com/news/press_releases/press_release.jsp?ymd=20070607&content_id=2011816&vkey=pr_mil&fext=.jsp&c_id=mil; "Dock Ellis pitched a no-hitter on LSD?" Snopes. June 12, 2015. By David Mikkelson. http://www.snopes.com/sports/baseball/ellis.asp

79. **Flying Blind:** "Airway Beacons/Unicoms" Montana.gov. http://www.mdt.mt.gov/aviation/beacons.shtml; "Arrows Across America" dreamsmithphotos.com. http://www.dreamsmithphotos.com/arrow/arrows.html; "Why is America dotted with giant, concrete arrows?" Citylab. Feb. 13, 2015. By John Metcalfe. http://www.citylab.com/work/2015/02/why-is-america-dotted-with-giant-concrete-arrows/385472/

80. **Guiding Light:** "Centennial Light" http://www.centennialbulb.org/

81. **The Japanese Attack on Omaha:** "May 5, 1945: Japanese balloon bomb kills 6 in Oregon" *Wired.* May 5, 2010. By David Kravets. https://www.wired.com/2010/05/0505japanese-balloon-kills-oregon/; "Beware of Japanese balloon bombs" NPR. Jan. 20, 2015. By Linton Weeks. http://www.npr.org/sections/npr-history-dept/2015/01/20/375820191/beware-of-japanese-balloon-bombs; "Military unit blows WWII-era Japanese balloon bomb to 'smithereens'" *The Globe and Mail.* Oct. 10, 2014. http://www.theglobeandmail.com/news/british-columbia/object-found-in-forest-may-be-second-world-war-era-japanese-balloon-bomb/article21065545/; "Dundee-Memorial Park Association" http://www.dundee-memorialpark.org/services-projects/

82. **The Longest Road Trip:** "Harlem Globetrotters play their first game" History.com. http://www.history.com/this-day-in-history/harlem-globetrotters-play-their-first-game; "Our story" Harlem Globetrotters. http://www.harlemglobetrotters.com/about/our-story; "An upset that shook the globe" *Hartford Courant.* Mar. 19, 2000. By Tom Condon; "Globetrotters lose by eliminating

the Generals" *Orlando Sentinel.* Aug. 14, 2015. By David Whitley; "The Washington Generals infamous 1971 win" Washington Generals Fan Blog. June 7, 2011. By Dan. http://washingtongeneralsfan.blogspot.com/2011/06/washington-generals-infamous-1971-win.html; "Meet the 10 honorary Harlem Globetrotters" *Mental Floss.* By Stacy Conradt. http://mentalfloss.com/article/74714/meet-10-honorary-harlem-globetrotters

83. **Playing with Fission:** "The radioactive Boy Scout" *Harper's Magazine.* Nov. 1998. By Ken Silverstein. http://harpers.org/archive/1998/11/the-radioactive-boy-scout/; "Man who tried to build a homemade nuclear reactor didn't die of radiation poisoning" *Ars Technica.* Mar. 14, 2017. By Cyrus Farivar. https://arstechnica.com/tech-policy/2017/03/radioactive-boy-scout-died-of-alcohol-poisoning-not-radiation-father-says/; "These men were caught building homemade nuclear reactors" *Gizmodo.* Aug. 3, 2011. By Kelly. http://gizmodo.com/5827565/these-men-were-caught-building-homemade-nuclear-reactors

84. **Carbonation Bubble:** "A massive lake of molten carbon the size of Mexico was just discovered under the US" *Forbes.* Apr. 30, 2017. By Trevor Nace; "Supervolcanoes" BBC. http://www.bbc.co.uk/science/earth/natural_disasters/supervolcano; "Scientists discover massive new magma chamber under Yellowstone" NPR. Apr. 24, 2015. By Scott Neuman. http://www.npr.org/sections/thetwo-way/2015/04/24/402032765/scientists-discover-massive-new-magma-chamber-under-yellowstone

85. **Bombs Away!:** "Boise City to celebrate 1943 bombing misguided B-17 crew sought" *The Oklahoman.* Nov. 21, 1990; "No. 2498 Sturzkampfflugzeug". University of Houston. By John H. Lienhard. http://www.uh.edu/engines/epi2498.htm; "The secret history of the Oklahoma Panhandle. *Conde Nast Traveler.* Aug. 4, 2015. By Ken Jennings. http://www.cntraveler.com/stories/2015-08-04/the-secret-history-of-the-oklahoma-panhandle

86. **Shining Through:** "Chief engineer explains the method behind the memorial" Anthem Community Council. Jan. 20, 2016. http://www.onlineatanthem.com/news/memorial-science; Anthem Veterans Memorial. http://onlineatanthem.com/sites/default/files/page-attachments/AVMBrochure.pdf

87. **The Real Rhode Island:** "Historical Information" RI.gov. https://www.ri.gov/facts/history.php; "Rhode Island history" Secretary of State's Office. http://sos.ri.gov/divisions/Civics-And-Education/RI-History; "The History and Future of Narragansett Bay" by Capers Jones, 2006. Boca Raton, Fla.: Universal Publishers. p. 170

88. **Keep on Truckin':** "Iowa 80" https://iowa80truckstop.com/

89. **The Secret Life of Nutmeg:** "What is a Nutmegger?" WNPR. Aug. 12, 2011. By Rebecca Furer. http://wnpr.org/post/what-nutmegger

ADDITIONAL PHOTO CREDITS

7. Photo title: nsa-museum-cm5-dsc02722, Photo title: nsa-museum-enigma-dsc02714, Photo title: nsa-museum-us-navy-cryptanalytic-bombe-dsc02716

21. Photo title: Property of the Hess Estate

28. Photo title: Future Birthplace of Captain James T. Kirk

30. Photo title: Dallas Mavericks 2014, Photo title: 1975? Ford Maverick, Photo title: McCain

33. Photo title: Decisions

38. Photo Title: Molasses Tank Explosion Injures 30 and kills 11 (*Boston Daily Globe*, January 16, 1919)

39. Photo Title: Maryland State Flag

47. Photo title: Ben Lomond

49. Photo title: Graffiti Highway, Centralia, PA

58. Photo title: Berkeley Pit 1991 near Butte, MT

62. Photo title: "Uncle Sam" Wilson (1766-1854) Grave–Oakwood Cemetery Troy (NY) 2015

66. Photo title: The Leaning Tower of Niles

72. Photo title: The Wiener's Circle, Chicago, Illinois

77. Photo title: Seattle Gum Wall

78. Photo title: Baseball from High Above Home

80. Photo title: 2012-03-08-13-35-43

82. Photo title: 20140713 72 BNSF Hinckley, Illinois

86. Photo title: Anthem's Veterans Memorial

87. Photo title: Welcome to Rhode Island

INDEX

217